The Witch by Thomas Middleton

The Witch has survived in quarto in the hand of Ralph Crane, a scrivener employed by the King's Players. From the dedication, it is traditionally believed that Middleton recovered the play from the King's Players at the Blackfriars Theater "not without much difficulty" because the play was a failure and lay in "an imprisoned obscurity."

Thomas Middleton was born in London in April 1580 and baptised on 18th April.

Middleton was aged only five when his father died. His mother remarried but this unfortunately fell apart into a fifteen year legal dispute regarding the inheritance due Thomas and his younger sister.

By the time he left Oxford, at the turn of the Century, Middleton had and published Microcynicon: Six Snarling Satirese which was denounced by the Archbishop of Canterbury and publicly burned.

In the early years of the 17th century, Middleton wrote topical pamphlets. One – Penniless Parliament of Threadbare Poets was reprinted several times and the subject of a parliamentary inquiry.

These early years writing plays continued to attract controversy. His writing partnership with Thomas Dekker brought him into conflict with Ben Jonson and George Chapman in the so-called War of the Theatres.

His finest work with Dekker was undoubtedly The Roaring Girl, a biography of the notorious Mary Frith.

In the 1610s, Middleton began another playwriting partnership, this time with the actor William Rowley, producing another slew of plays including Wit at Several Weapons and A Fair Quarrel.

The ever adaptable Middleton seemed at ease working with others or by himself. His solo writing credits include the comic masterpiece, A Chaste Maid in Cheapside, in 1613.

In 1620 he was officially appointed as chronologer of the City of London, a post he held until his death.

The 1620s saw the production of his and Rowley's tragedy, and continual favourite, The Changeling, and of several other tragicomedies.

However in 1624, he reached a peak of notoriety when his dramatic allegory A Game at Chess was staged by the King's Men. Though Middleton's approach was strongly patriotic, the Privy Council silenced the play after only nine performances at the Globe theatre, having received a complaint from the Spanish ambassador.

What happened next is a mystery. It is the last play recorded as having being written by Middleton.

Thomas Middleton died at his home at Newington Butts in Southwark in the summer of 1627, and was buried on July 4th, in St Mary's churchyard which today survives as a public park in Elephant and Castle.

Index of Contents

DRAMATIS PERSONAE
DUKE
LORD GOVERNOR
SEBASTIAN, contracted to ISABELLA
FERNANDO, his friend
ANTONIO, husband to ISABELLA
ABBERZANES, a gentleman, neither honest, wise, nor valiant
ALMACHILDES, a fantastical gentleman
GASPERO   }
HERMIO   } servants to ANTONIO
FIRESTONE, the clown and Hecate's son
BOY
DUCHESS
ISABELLA, niece to the GOVERNOR and wife to ANTONIO
FRANCISCA, Antonio's sister
AMORETTA, the Duchess's woman
FLORIDA, a courtesan
An OLD WOMAN
HECATE, the chief witch
Five other witches, including STADLIN, HOPPO, PUCKLE and HELLWAIN

MALKIN, a spirit like a cat
Other Witches and Servants, Mutes

To the truly worthy and generously affected Thomas Holmes, Esquire:

Noble Sir,

As a true testimony of my ready inclination to your service, I have, merely upon a taste of your desire, recovered into my hands, though not without much difficulty, this ignorantly ill-fated labour of mine. Witches are, ipso facto, by the law condemn'd, and it only, I think, hath made her lie so long in an imprison'd obscurity. For your sake alone, she hath thus far conjur'd herself abroad, and bears no other charms about her but what may tend to your recreation, nor no other spell but to possess you with a belief that as she, so he that first taught her to enchant, will always be

Your devoted

Thomas Middleton

ACT I

SCENE I - The Grounds of the Lord Governor's House, a Banquet Laid Out

Enter **SEBASTIAN** and **FERNANDO**.

SEBASTIAN
My three years spent in war has now undone
My peace forever.

FERNANDO
Good, be patient, sir.

SEBASTIAN
She is my wife by contract before heaven
And all the angels, sir.

FERNANDO
I do believe you;
But where's the remedy now? You see she's gone:
Another has possession.

SEBASTIAN
There's the torment.

FERNANDO

This day, being the first of your return,
Unluckily proves the first too of her fastening.
Her uncle, sir, the **GOVERNOR** of Ravenna,
Holding a good opinion of the bridegroom,
As he's fair-spoken, sir, and wondrous mild—

SEBASTIAN
There goes the devil in a sheepskin!

FERNANDO
With all speed,
Clapp'd it up suddenly. I cannot think, sure,
That the maid overloves him; though being married
Perhaps, for her own credit, now she intends
Performance of an honest, duteous wife.

SEBASTIAN
Sir, I've a world of business. Question nothing;
You will but lose your labour. 'Tis not fit
For any, hardly mine own secrecy,
To know what I intend. I take my leave, sir.
I find such strange employments in myself
That, unless death pity me and lay me down,
I shall not sleep these seven years. That's the least, sir.

[Exit.

FERNANDO
That sorrow's dangerous can abide no counsel.
'Tis like a wound past cure; wrongs done to love
Strike the heart deeply. None can truly judge on't
But the poor, sensible sufferer, whom it racks
With unbelieved pains, which men in health,
That enjoy love, not possibly can act,
Nay, not so much as think. In troth, I pity him;
His sighs drink life-blood in this time of feasting.
A banquet towards, too? Not yet hath riot
Play'd out her last scene? At such entertainments still
Forgetfulness obeys, and surfeit governs;
Here's marriage sweetly honour'd in gorg'd stomachs,
And overflowing cups.

[Enter **GASPERO** and **SERVANT**.

GASPERO
Where is she, sirrah?

SERVANT

Not far off.

GASPERO
Prithee, where? Go fetch her hither;
I'll rid him away straight.

[Exit **SERVANT**.

The Duke's now risen, sir.

FERNANDO
I am a joyful man to hear it, sir;
It seems h'as drunk the less, though I think he
That has the least, h'as certainly enough.

[Exit.

GASPERO
I have observ'd this fellow: all the feast-time,
He hath not pledg'd one cup, but look'd most wickedly
Upon good Malaga, flies to the blackjack still,
And sticks to small drink like a water rat.

[Enter **FLORIDA**.

[Aside] Oh, here she comes. Alas, the poor whore weeps:
'Tis not for grace now, all the world must judge,
It is for spleen and madness 'gainst this marriage.
I do but think but how she could beat the vicar now,
Scratch the man horribly that gave the woman,
The woman worst of all, if she durst do it.—
Why, how now, mistress? This weeping needs not, for though
My master marry for his reputation,
He means to keep you, too.

FLORIDA
How, sir?

GASPERO
He doth, indeed;
He swore 't to me last night. Are you so simple,
And have been five years traded, as to think
One woman would serve him? Fie, not an empress!
Why, he'll be sick o' th' wife within ten nights,
Or never trust my judgment.

FLORIDA
Will he, think'st thou?

GASPERO
Will he!

FLORIDA
I find thee still so comfortable;
Beshrew my heart if I knew how to miss thee.
They talk to gentlemen, perfumers, and such things;
Give me the kindness of the master's man
In my distress, say I.

GASPERO
'Tis your great love, forsooth.
Please you withdraw yourself to yond private parlour:
I'll send you venison, custard, parsnip pie;
For banqueting stuff, as suckets, jellies, syrups,
I will bring in myself.

FLORIDA
I'll take 'em kindly, sir.

[Exit.

GASPERO
Sh'as your grand strumpet's complement to a tittle:
'Tis a fair building; it had need. It has
Just at this time some one and twenty inmates;
But half of 'em are young merchants, they'll depart shortly:
They take but rooms for summer, and away they,
When 't grows foul weather. Marry, then come the termers,
And commonly they're well-booted for all seasons.

[Enter **ALMACHILDES** and **AMORETTA**.

But peace, no more: the guests are coming in.

[Withdraws.

ALMACHILDES
The fates have bless'd me; have I met you privately?

AMORETTA
Why, sir; why, Almachildes!

ALMACHILDES
Not a kiss?

AMORETTA

I'll call aloud, i'faith.

ALMACHILDES
I'll stop your mouth.

AMORETTA
Upon my love to reputation,
I'll tell the Duchess once more.

ALMACHILDES
'Tis the way
To make her laugh a little.

AMORETTA
She'll not think
That you dare use a maid of honour thus.

ALMACHILDES
Amsterdam swallow thee for a puritan
And Geneva cast thee up again, like she that sunk
At Charing Cross and rose again at Queenhithe!

AMORETTA
Ay, these are the holy fruits of the sweet vine, sir.

[She leaves him.

ALMACHILDES [Aside]
Sweet venery be with thee, and I at the tail of my wish: I am a little headstrong, and so are most of the company. I will to the witches: they say they have charms and tricks to make a wench fall backwards, and lead a man herself to a country house some mile out of the town, like a firedrake. There be such whoreson kind girls, and such bawdy witches, and I'll try conclusions.

[Enter **DUKE**, **DUCHESS**, Lord **GOVERNOR**, **ANTONIO**, and **ISABELLA**, **FRANCISCA**.

DUKE
A banquet yet? Why, surely, my lord Governor,
Bacchus could never boast of a day till now
To spread his power, and make his glory known.

DUCHESS
Sir, y'have done nobly, though in modesty
You keep it from us; know we understand so much
All this day's cost 'tis your great love bestows
In honour of the bride, your virtuous niece.

GOVERNOR
In love to goodness and your presence, madam,

So understood, 'tis rightly.

DUKE
Now will I
Have a strange health after all these.

GOVERNOR
What's that, my lord?

DUKE
A health in a strange cup, and 't shall go round.

GOVERNOR
Your grace need not doubt that, sir, having seen
So many pledg'd already; this fair company
Cannot shrink now for one, so it end there.

DUKE
It shall, for all ends here; here's a full period.

[Brings forth a skull.

GOVERNOR
A skull, my lord?

DUKE
Call it a soldier's cup, man.
Fie, how you fright the women! I have sworn
It shall go round, excepting only you, sir,
For your late sickness, and the bride herself,
Whose health it is.

ISABELLA
Marry, I thank heaven for that.

DUKE
Our Duchess I know will pledge us, though the cup
Was once her father's head, which as a trophy
We'll keep till death, in memory of that conquest.
He was the greatest foe our steel e'er strook at,
And he was bravely slain. Then took we thee
Into our bosom's love; thou madest the peace
For all thy country: thou, that beauty did.
We're dearer than a father, are we not?

DUCHESS
Yes, sir, by much.

DUKE
And we shall find that straight.

ANTONIO
That's an ill bride-cup for a marriage-day;
I do not like the fate on't.

GOVERNOR
Good my lord,
The Duchess looks pale; let her not pledge you there.

DUKE
Pale?

DUCHESS
Sir, not I.

DUKE
See how your lordship fails now,
The rose not fresher, nor the sun at rising
More comfortably pleasing.

DUCHESS [To **ANTONIO**]
Sir, to you,
The lord of this day's honour.

ANTONIO
All first moving
From your grace, madam, and the duke's great favour.
[To **FRANCISCA**] Sister, it must.

FRANCISCA [Aside]
This the worst fright that could come
To a conceal'd great belly: I'm with child,
And this will bring it out, or make me come
Some seven weeks sooner than we maidens reckon.

DUCHESS [Aside]
Did ever cruel, barbarous act match this?
Twice hath his surfeits brought my father's memory
Thus spitefully and scornfully to mine eyes,
And I'll endure 't no more; 'tis in my heart since:
I'll be reveng'd, as far as death can lead me.

ALMACHILDES [Aside]
Am I the last man then? I may deserve
To be the first one day.

GOVERNOR [To **DUKE**]
Sir, it has gone round now.

DUKE
The round? An excellent way to train up soldiers.
Where's the bride and bridegroom?

ANTONIO
At your happy service.

DUKE
A boy tonight at least: I charge you look to't
Or I'll renounce you for industrious subjects.

ANTONIO
Your grace speaks like a worthy and tried soldier.

[Exeunt all except **GASPERO**.

GASPERO
And you'll do well, for one that ne'er toss'd pike, sir.

[Exit.

SCENE II - Hecate's Cave

Enter **HECATE** and other **WITCHES** with properties and habits fitting.

HECATE
Titty and Tiffin, Suckin and Pidgen, Liard and Robin,
White spirits, black spirits, grey spirits, red spirits,
Devil-toad, devil-ram, devil-cat, and devil-dam!
Why, Hoppo and Stadlin, Hellwain and Puckle!

STADLIN [Within]
Here, sweating at the vessel.

HECATE
Boil it well.

HOPPO [Within]
It gallops now.

HECATE
Are the flames blue enough,

Or shall I use a little seething more?

STADLIN [Within]
The nips of fairies upon maid's white hips
Are not more perfect azure.

HECATE
Tend it carefully.
Send Stadlin to me with a brazen dish
That I may fall to work upon these serpents
And squeeze 'em ready for the second hour.
Why, when?

[Enter **STADLIN** with a dish.]

STADLIN
Here's Stadlin and the dish.

HECATE [Giving her a dead child's **BODY**]
Here, take this unbaptised brat.
Boil it well, preserve the fat:
You know 'tis precious to transfer
Our 'nointed flesh into the air
In moonlight nights o'er steeple tops,
Mountains and pine trees, that like pricks or stops
Seem to our height; high towers and roofs of princes
Like wrinkles in the earth: whole provinces
Appear to our sight then ev'n leek
A russet mole upon some lady's cheek.
When hundred leagues in air, we feast, and sing.
Dance, kiss, and coll, use everything.
What young man can we wish to pleasure us
But we enjoy him in an incubus?
Thou know'st it, Stadlin?

STADLIN
Usually that's done.

HECATE
Last night thou got'st the Major of Whelplie's son;
I knew him by his black cloak, lin'd with yallow.
I think thou'st spoil'd the youth: he's but seventeen;
I'll have him the next mounting. Away, in;
Go feed the vessel for the second hour.

STADLIN
Where be the magic herbs?

HECATE
They're down his throat:
His mouth cramm'd full, his ears and nostrils stuff'd.
I thrust in eleoselinum lately
Aconitum, frondes populeas, and soot—
You may see that, he looks so black i' th' mouth—
Then sium, acorum vulgare too,
Pentaphyllon, the blood of a flitter-mouse,
Solanum somnificum et oleum.

STADLIN
Then there's all, Hecate?

HECATE
Is the heart of wax
Stuck full of magic needles?

STADLIN
'Tis done, Hecate.

HECATE
And is the farmer's picture, and his wife's,
Laid down to th' fire yet?

STADLIN
They're a-roasting both, too.

HECATE
Good.

[Exit **STADLIN**.

Then their marrows are a-melting subtly,
And three months' sickness sucks up life in 'em.
They denied me often flour, barm, and milk,
Goose-grease, and tar, when I ne'er hurt their churnings,
Their brew locks, nor their batches, nor forspoke
Any of their breedings. Now I'll be meet with 'em.
Seven of their young pigs I have bewitch'd already
Of their last litter,
Nine ducklings, thirteen goslings, and a hog
Fell lame last Sunday after Evensong, too.
And mark how their sheep prosper, or what sup
Each milch-kine gives to th' pail. I'll send those snakes
Shall milk 'em all beforehand:
The dew-skirted dairy wenches
Shall stroke dry dugs for this, and go home cursing.
I'll mar their sillabubs and frothy feastings

Under cows' bellies with the parish youths.
Where's Firestone? Our son Firestone?

[Enter **FIRESTONE**.

FIRESTONE
Here I am, mother.

HECATE
Take in this brazen dish full of dear ware,
Thou shalt have all when I die; and that will be
Ev'n just at twelve a'clock at night, come three year.

FIRESTONE
And may you not have one a'clock in to th' dozen, mother?

HECATE
No.

FIRESTONE
Your spirits are then more unconscionable than bakers. You'll have liv'd then, mother, sixscore year to the hundred; and methinks after sixscore years, the devil might give you a cast, for he's a fruiterer too, and has been from the beginning. The first apple that e'er was eaten came through his fingers: the costermonger's then I hold to be the ancientest trade, though some would have the tailor prick'd down before him.

HECATE
Go, and take heed you shed not by the way.
The hour must have her portion: 'tis dear syrup;
Each charmed drop is able to confound
A family consisting of nineteen,
Or one and twenty feeders.

FIRESTONE
Marry, here's stuff indeed!
Dear syrup call you it? [Aside] A little thing
Would make me give you a dram on't in a posset
And cut you three years shorter.

HECATE
Thou'rt now
About some villainy?

FIRESTONE
Not I, forsooth.
[Aside] Truly the devil's in her, I think. How one villain smells out another straight! There's no knavery but is nos'd like a dog, and can smell out a dog's meaning.—Mother, I pray give me leave to ramble abroad tonight with the night-mare, for I have a great mind to overlay a fat parson's daughter.

HECATE
And who shall lie with me then?

FIRESTONE
The great cat.
For one night, mother, 'tis but a night;
Make shift with him for once.

HECATE
You're a kind son,
But 'tis the nature of you all, I see that:
You had rather hunt after strange women still
Than lie with your own mothers. Get thee gone,
Sweat thy six ounces out about the vessel
And thou shalt play at midnight; the night-mare
Shall call thee when it walks.

FIRESTONE
Thanks, most sweet mother.

[Exit. Enter **SEBASTIAN**.

HECATE
Urchins, elves, hags, satyrs, pans, fawns, silens, kit with the candlestick, tritons, centaurs, dwarfs, imps, the spoorn, the mare, the man i' th' oak, the hellwain, the firedrake, the puckle! A ab hur hus!

SEBASTIAN [Aside]
Heaven knows with what unwillingness and hate
I enter this damn'd place. But such extremes
Of wrongs in love fight 'gainst religious knowledge,
That were I led by this disease to deaths
As numberless as creatures that must die,
I could not shun the way. I know what 'tis
To pity madmen now; they're wretched things
That ever were created, if they be
Of woman's making and her faithless vows.
I fear they're now a-kissing. What's a'clock?
'Tis now but suppertime, but night will come,
And all new-married couples make short suppers.—
Whate'er thou art, I have no spare time to fear thee;
My horrors are so strong and great already
That thou seem'st nothing. Up and laze not;
Hadst thou my business, thou couldst ne'er sit so:
'Twould firk thee into air a thousand mile
Beyond thy ointments. I would I were read
So much in thy black power as mine own griefs.
I'm in great need of help: wilt give me any?

HECATE
Thy boldness takes me bravely. We are all sworn
To sweat for such a spirit. See, I regard thee;
I rise and bid thee welcome. What's thy wish now?

SEBASTIAN
Oh, my heart swells with't! I must take breath first.

HECATE
Is't to confound some enemy on the seas?
It may be done tonight. Stadlin's within;
She raises all your sudden ruinous storms
That shipwrack barks and tears up growing oaks,
Flies over houses and takes Anno Domini
Out of a rich man's chimney—a sweet place for't!
He would be hang'd ere he would set his own years there;
They must be chamber'd in a five-pound picture,
A green silk curtain drawn before the eyes on't.
His rotten, diseas'd years! Or dost thou envy
The fat prosperity of any neighbour?
I'll call forth Hoppo, and her incantation
Can straight destroy the young of all his cattle,
Blast vineyards, orchards, meadows, or in one night
Transport his dung, hay, corn by reeks, whole stacks,
Into thine own ground.

SEBASTIAN
This would come most richly now
To many a country grazier. But my envy
Lies not so low as cattle, corn, or vines:
'Twill trouble your best powers to give me ease.

HECATE
Is it to starve up generation?
To strike a barrenness in man or woman?

SEBASTIAN
Hah?

HECATE
Hah? Did you feel me there? I knew your grief.

SEBASTIAN
Can there be such things done?

HECATE
Are these the skins

Of serpents? These of snakes?

SEBASTIAN
I see they are.

HECATE [Giving him skins]
So sure into what house these are convey'd,
Knit with these charmed and retentive knots,
Neither the man begets nor woman breeds;
No, nor performs the least desires of wedlock,
Being then a mutual duty. I could give thee
Chirocineta, adincantida,
Archimedon, marmaritin, calicia,
Which I could sort to villainous, barren ends,
But this leads the same way. More I could instance,
As the same needles thrust into their pillows
That sews and socks up dead men in their sheets,
A privy gristle of a man that hangs
After sunset. Good, excellent; yet all's there, sir.

SEBASTIAN
You could not do a man that special kindness
To part 'em utterly now? Could you do that?

HECATE
No, time must do't. We cannot disjoin wedlock:
'Tis of heaven's fast'ning; well may we raise jars,
Jealousies, strifes, and heart-burning disagreements,
Like a thick scurf o'er life, as did our master
Upon that patient miracle, but the work itself
Our power cannot disjoint.

SEBASTIAN
I depart happy
In what I have then, being constrained to this.
[Aside] And grant, you greater powers that dispose men,
That I may never need this hag again.

[Exit.

HECATE
I know he loves me not, nor there's no hope on't;
'Tis for the love of mischief I do this,
And that we're sworn to, the first oath we take.

[Enter **FIRESTONE**.

FIRESTONE

Oh mother, mother!

HECATE
What the news with thee now?

FIRESTONE
There's the bravest young gentleman within, and the fineliest drunk; I thought he would have fall'n into the vessel. He stumbled at a pipkin of child's grease, reel'd against Stadlin, overthrew her, and in the tumbling cast, struck up old Puckle's heels with her clothes over her ears.

HECATE
Hoyday!

FIRESTONE
I was fain to throw the cat upon her to save her honesty, and all little enough: I cried out still, "I pray be covered!" See where he comes now, mother.

[Enter **ALMACHILDES**.

ALMACHILDES
Call you these witches?
They be tumblers, methinks, very flat tumblers.

HECATE [Aside]
'Tis **ALMACHILDES**: fresh blood stirs in me,
The man that I have lusted to enjoy;
I have had him thrice in incubus already.

ALMACHILDES
Is your name Goody Hag?

HECATE
'Tis anything.
Call me the horrid'st and unhallowed'st things
That life and nature trembles at, for thee
I'll be the same. Thou com'st for a love charm now?

ALMACHILDES
Why, thou'rt a witch, I think.

HECATE
Thou shalt have a choice
Of twenty, wet or dry.

ALMACHILDES
Nay, let's have dry ones.

HECATE

If thou wilt use't by way of cup and potion,
I'll give thee a remora shall bewitch her straight.

ALMACHILDES
A remora? What's that?

HECATE
A little suck-stone;
Some call it a sea-lamprey, a small fish.

ALMACHILDES
And must be butter'd?

HECATE
The bones of a green frog, too, wondrous precious,
The flesh consumed by pismires.

ALMACHILDES
Pismires? Give me a chamberpot.

FIRESTONE [Aside]
You shall see him go nigh to be so unmannerly, he'll make water before my mother anon.

ALMACHILDES
And now you talk of frogs, I have somewhat here;
I come not empty-pocketed from a banquet.
I learn'd that of my haberdasher's wife.
Look, Goody Witch, there's a toad in marchpane for you.

[Gives her marchpane.

HECATE
Oh sir, you have fitted me.

ALMACHILDES
And here's a spawn or two
Of the same paddock brood, too, for your son.

[Gives him marchpane.

FIRESTONE
I thank your worship, sir; how comes your handkercher so sweetly thus beray'd? Sure 'tis wet sucket, sir.

ALMACHILDES
'Tis nothing but the syrup the toad spit.
Take all, I prithee.

HECATE

That was kindly done, sir;
And you shall sup with me tonight for this.

ALMACHILDES
How? Sup with thee? Dost think I'll eat fried rats
And pickled spiders?

HECATE
No, I can command, sir,
The best meat i' th' whole province for my friends,
And reverently serv'd in, too.

ALMACHILDES
How?

HECATE
In good fashion.

ALMACHILDES
Let me but see that, and I'll sup with you.

[She conjures; and enter a cat playing on a fiddle and spirits with meat.

The cat and fiddle? An excellent ordinary.
You had a devil once, in a fox skin?

HECATE
Oh, I have him still. Come, walk with me, sir.

[Exeunt all but **FIRESTONE**.

FIRESTONE
How apt and ready is a drunkard now to reel to the devil! Well, I'll even in and see how he eats, and I'll be hang'd if I be not the fatter of the twain with laughing at him.

[Exit.

ACT II

SCENE I - Antonio's House

Enter **ANTONIO** and **GASPERO**.

GASPERO
Good sir, whence springs this sadness? Trust me, sir,
You look not like a man was married yesterday.

There could come no ill tidings since last night
To cause that discontent. I was wont to know all
Before you had a wife, sir; you ne'er found me
Without those parts of manhood: trust and secrecy.

ANTONIO
I will not tell thee this.

GASPERO
Not your true servant, sir?

ANTONIO
True? You'll all flout according to your talent,
The best a man can keep of you; and a hell 'tis
For masters to pay wages to be laugh'd at.
Give order that two cocks be boiled to jelly.

GASPERO
How? Two cocks boil'd to jelly?

ANTONIO
Fetch half an ounce of pearl.

[Exit.

GASPERO
This is a cullis
For a consumption, and I hope one night
Has not brought you to need the cook already,
And some part of the goldsmith: what, two trades
In four and twenty hours, and less time?
Pray heaven the surgeon and the pothecary
Keep out, and then 'tis well. You had better fortune,
As far as I see, with your strumpet sojourner,
Your little four-nobles-a-week: I ne'er knew you
Eat one panada all the time y'have kept her,
And is't in one night now, come up to two-cock broth?
I wonder at the alteration strangely.

[Enter **FRANCISCA**.

FRANCISCA
Good morrow, Gasper.

GASPERO
Your hearty wishes, mistress,
And your sweet dreams come upon you.

FRANCISCA
What that, sir?

GASPERO
In a good husband, that's my real meaning.

FRANCISCA
Saw you my brother lately?

GASPERO
Yes.

FRANCISCA
I met him now
As sad, methought, as grief could make a man;
Know you the cause?

GASPERO
Not I: I know nothing
But half an ounce of pearl, and kitchen-business
Which I will see perform'd with all fidelity;
I'll break my trust in nothing: not in porridge, I.

[Exit.

FRANCISCA
I have the hardest fortune, I think, of a hundred
Gentlewomen; some can make merry with a friend seven year,
And nothing seen, as perfect a maid still,
To the world's knowledge, as she came from rocking.
But 'twas my luck, at the first hour forsooth,
To prove too fruitful: sure I'm near my time.
I'm yet but a young scholar, I may fail
In my account; but certainly I do not.
These bastards come upon poor venturing gentlewomen ten to one faster than your legitimate children.
If I had been married, I'll be hanged if I had been with child so soon now. When they are once husbands,
they'll be whipp'd ere they take such pains as a friend will do, to come by water to the back door at
midnight, there stay perhaps an hour in all weathers, with a pair of reeking watermen, laden with
bottles of wine, chewets, and currant custards. I may curse those egg pies; they are meat that help
forward too fast.
This hath been usual with me, night by night,
Honesty forgive me, when my brother hath been
Dreaming of no such junkets, yet he hath far'd
The better for my sake, though he little think
For what, nor must he ever. My friend promis'd me
To provide safely for me, and devise
A means to save my credit here i' th' house.
My brother sure would kill me if he knew't,

And powder up my friend, and all his kindred,
For an East Indian voyage.

[Enter **ISABELLA**.

ISABELLA
Alone, sister?

FRANCISCA [Aside]
No, there's another with me, though you see't not.—
Morrow, sweet sister, how have you slept tonight?

ISABELLA
More than I thought I should; I've had good rest.

FRANCISCA
I'm glad to hear't.

ISABELLA
Sister, methinks you are too long alone,
And lose much good time, sociable and honest;
I'm for the married life, I must praise that now.

FRANCISCA
I cannot blame you, sister, to commend it.
You have happen'd well, no doubt, on a kind husband,
And that's not every woman's fortune, sister,
You know if he were any but my brother
My praises should not leave him yet so soon.

ISABELLA
I must acknowledge, sister, that my life
Is happily bless'd with him: he is no gamester
That ever I could find or hear of yet,
Nor midnight surfeiter; he does intend
To leave tobacco, too.

FRANCISCA
Why, here's a husband!

ISABELLA
He saw it did offend me, and swore freely
He'll ne'er take pleasure in a toy again
That should displease me: some knights' wives in town
Will have great hope, upon his reformation,
To bring their husbands' breaths into th' old fashion,
And make 'em kiss like Christians, not like pagans.

FRANCISCA
I promise you, sister, 'twill be a worthy work
To put down all these pipers; 'tis a great pity
There should not be a statute against them,
As against fiddlers.

ISABELLA
These good offices,
If you had a husband, you might exercise
To th' good o' th' commonwealth, and do much profit:
Beside, it is a comfort to a woman
T'have children, sister, a great blessing certainly.

FRANCISCA
They will come fast enough.

ISABELLA
Not so fast neither,
As they're still welcome to an honest woman.

FRANCISCA [Aside]
How near she comes to me! I protest she grates
My very skin.

ISABELLA
Were I conceiv'd with child,
Beshrew my heart, I should be so proud on't.

FRANCISCA
That's natural: pride is a kind of swelling;
[Aside] And yet I've small cause to be proud of mine.

ISABELLA
You are no good companion for a wife:
Get you a husband; prithee, sister, do,
That I may ask your counsel now and then.
'Twill mend you discourse much: you maids know nothing.

FRANCISCA
No, we are fools, but commonly we prove
Quicker mothers than you that have husbands.
[Aside] I'm sure I shall else; I may speak for one.

[Enter **ANTONIO**.

ANTONIO [Aside]
I will not look upon her: I'll pass by
And make as though I see her not.

ISABELLA
Why sir,
Pray your opinion, by the way, with leave, sir:
I'm counselling your sister here to marry.

ANTONIO
To marry? Soft, the priest is not at leisure yet:
Some five years hence. Would you fain marry, sister?

FRANCISCA
I have no such hunger to't, sir, [Aside] for I think
I've a good bit that well may stay my stomach
As well as any that broke fast a sinner.

ANTONIO
Though she seem tall of growth, she's short in years
Of some that seem much lower. How old, sister?
Not seventeen, for a yard of lawn?

FRANCISCA
Not yet, sir.

ANTONIO
I told you so.

FRANCISCA [Aside]
I would he'd laid a wager of old shirts rather,
I shall have more need of them shortly: and yet
A yard of lawn will serve for a christening-cloth.
I have a use for everything, as my case stands.

ISABELLA
I care not if I try my voice this morning,
But I have got a cold, sir, by your means.

ANTONIO
I'll strive to mean that fault.

ISABELLA
I thank you sir.

Song

In a maiden-time profess'd,
Then we say that life is best.
Tasting once the married life,
Then we only praise the wife.

There's but one state more to try
Which makes women laugh or cry:
Widow, widow. Of these three,
The middle's best, and that give me.

ANTONIO [Kissing her]
There's thy reward.

ISABELLA
I will not grumble, sir,
Like some musician; if more come, 'tis welcome.

FRANCISCA [Aside]
Such tricks have made me do all that I have done;
Your kissing married folks spoil all the maids that ever live i' th' house with 'em.

[Enter **ABBERZANES** with his servants carrying packages and bottles.

Oh, here he comes with his bags and bottles; he was born to lead poor watermen, and I.

ABBERZANES
Go, fellows, into the larder, let the bake-meats be sorted by themselves.

ANTONIO
Why, sir—

ABBERZANES
Look the canary bottles be well-stopp'd,
The three of claret shall be drunk at dinner.

[Exit Abberzanes' **SERVANTS**.

ANTONIO
My good sir, y'are too plenteous of these courtesies,
Indeed you are; forbear 'em, I beseech ye.
I know no merit in me but poor love
And a true friend's well-wishing that can cause
This kindness in excess. [Aside] I' th' state that I am,
I shall go near to kick this fellow shortly
And send him downstairs with his bag and baggage.
Why comes he now I'm married? There's the point.—
I pray, forbear these things.

ABBERZANES
Alas, you know, sir,
These idle toys, which you call courtesies,
They cost me nothing but my servants' travail.
One office must be kind, sir, to another,

You know the fashion. What, the gentlewoman
Your sister's sad, methinks.

ANTONIO
I know no cause she has.

FRANCISCA [Aside]
Nor shall, by my good will.

[She takes **ABBERZANES** aside.

What do you mean, sir?
Shall I stay here to shame myself and you?
The time may be tonight, for aught you know.

ABBERZANES
Peace: there's means wrought, I tell thee.

FRANCISCA
Ay, sir, when?

[Enter **SEBASTIAN** disguised as Celio, a servant and **GENTLEMAN**.

ANTONIO
How now? What's he?

ISABELLA
Oh, this is the man, sir,
I entertain'd this morning for my service.
Please you to give your liking.

ANTONIO
Yes, he's welcome.
I like him not amiss. [To **SEBASTIAN**] Thou wouldst speak business,
Wouldst thou not?

SEBASTIAN
Yes; may it please you, sir,
There is a gentleman from the northern parts
Hath brought a letter, as it seems, in haste.

ANTONIO
From whom?

GENTLEMAN
Your bonny lady mother, sir.

ANTONIO

You're kindly welcome, sir: how doth she?

GENTLEMAN
I left her heal' varray well, sir.

ANTONIO [Takes the letter and reads.]
"I pray send your sister down all speed to me. I hope it will prove much for her good, in the way of her preferment. Fail me not, I desire you, son, nor let any excuse of hers withhold her; I have sent, ready furnish'd, horse and man for her."

ABBERZANES
Now have I thought upon you?

FRANCISCA
Peace, good sir,
You're worthy of a kindness another time.

ANTONIO
Her will shall be obey'd. Sister, prepare yourself;
You must down with all speed.

FRANCISCA
I know, down I must,
And good speed send me!

ANTONIO
'Tis our mother's pleasure.

FRANCISCA
Good sir, write back again, and certify her
I'm at my heart's wish here; I'm with my friends
And can be but well, say.

ANTONIO
You shall pardon me, sister;
I hold it no wise part to contradict her,
Nor would I counsel you to't.

FRANCISCA
'Tis so uncouth
Living i' th' country now I'm us'd to th' city
That I shall nev'r endure't.

ABBERZANES
Perhaps, forsooth,
'Tis not her meaning you shall live there long.
I do not think but after a month or so
You'll be sent up again: that's my conceit.

However, let her have her will.

ANTONIO
Ay, good sir,
Great reason 'tis she should.

ISABELLA
I am sorry, sister,
'Tis our hard fortune thus to part so soon.

FRANCISCA
The sorrow will be mine.

ANTONIO [To **GENTLEMAN**] Please you walk in, sir;
We'll have one health unto these northern parts,
Though I be sick at heart.

ABBERZANES
Ay, sir, a deep one—

Exeunt **ANTONIO, ISABELLA, and GENTLEMAN.**

[To **FRANCISCA**] Which you shall pledge, too.

FRANCISCA
You shall pardon me:
I have pledg'd one too deep already, sir.

ABBERZANES [Aside to her]
Peace; all's provided for: thy wine's laid in,
Sugar and spice, the place not ten mile hence.
What cause have maids now to complain of men,
When a farmhouse can make all whole again?

[Exeunt **ABBERZANES** and **FRANCISCA.**

SEBASTIAN
It takes: h'as no content; how well she bears it yet!
Hardly myself can find so much from her
That am acquainted with the cold disease.
O, honesty's a rare wealth in a woman!
It knows no want, at least will express none,
Not in a look. Yet I'm not throughly happy:
His ill does me no good; well may it keep me
From open rage and madness for a time,
But I feel heart's grief in the same place still.
What makes the greatest torment 'mongst lost souls?
'Tis not so much the horror of their pains,

Though they be infinite, as the loss of joys:
It is that deprivation is the mother
Of all the groans in hell, and here on earth
Of all the red sighs in the hearts of lovers.
Still she's not mine that can be no man's else
Till I be nothing, if religion
Have the same strength for me as 't has for others:
Holy vows witness that our souls were married.

[Enter **GASPERO** and Lord **GOVERNOR** attended by **GENTLEMAN**.

GASPERO
Where are you, sir? Come, pray give your attendance.
Here's my lord Governor come.

GOVERNOR
Where's our new kindred?
Not stirring yet, I think?

GASPERO
Yes, my good lord.
Please you walk near?

GOVERNOR
Come, gentlemen, we'll enter.

SEBASTIAN [Aside]
I ha' done't upon a breach; this a lesser venture.

[Exeunt.

SCENE II – The Duke's Palace

Enter **ALMACHILDES**.

ALMACHILDES
What a mad toy took me to sup with witches!
Fie of all drunken humours! By this hand,
I could beat myself when I think on't; and the rascals
Made me good cheer, too: and to my understanding then
Ate some of every dish, and spoil'd the rest.
But coming to my lodging, I remember
I was as hungry as a tired foot-post.
What's this?

[He takes a ribbon from his pocket.

Oh, 'tis the charm her hagship gave me
For my duchess' obstinate woman; wound about
A threepenny silk ribbon of three colours,
"Necte tribus nodis ternos Amoretta colores."
Amoretta: why there's her name indeed.
"Necte, Amoretta," again, two boughts,
"Nodo et Veneris dic vincula necte."
Nay, if Veneris be one, I'm sure there's no dead flesh in't.
If I should undertake to construe this now,
I should make a fine piece of work of it,
For few young gallants are given to good construction
Of anything, hardly of their best friends' wives,
Sisters, or nieces. Let me see what I can do now.
"Necte tribus nodis," Nick of the tribe of noddies, "ternos colores," that makes turn'd colours, "nodo et Veneris," goes to his venery like a noddy, "dic vincula," with Dick the vintner's boy. Here were a sweet charm now if this were the meaning on't, and very likely to overcome an honourable gentlewoman. The whoreson old hellcat would have given me the brain of a cat once in my handkercher—I bade her make sauce with't with a vengeance—and a little bone in the [nethermost] part of a wolf's tail—
I bade her pick her teeth with't with a pest'lence.
Nay, this is somewhat cleanly yet, and handsome.
A coloured ribbon? A fine, gentle charm;
A man may give't his sister, his brother's wife
Ordinarily.

[Enter **AMORETTA**.

See, here she comes luckily.

AMORETTA
Bless'd powers, what secret sin have I committed
That still you send this punishment upon me?

ALMACHILDES
'Tis but a gentle punishment, so take it.

[He clasps her and hides the charm on her.

AMORETTA
Why, sir, what mean you? Will you ravish me?

ALMACHILDES
What, in the gallery? And the sun peep in?
There's fitter time and place. [Aside] 'Tis in her bosom now.

AMORETTA
Go, you're the rudest thing e'er came at court.

ALMACHILDES [Aside]
Well, well, I hope you'll tell me another tale
Ere you be two hours older: a rude thing?
I'll make you eat your word; I'll make all split else.

[Exit.

AMORETTA
Nay, now I think on't better, I'm too blame, too.
There's not a sweeter gentleman in court:
Nobly descended, too, and dances well.
Beshrew my heart; I'll take him when there's time,
He will be catch'd up quickly. The Duchess says
Sh'as some employment for him, and has sworn me
To use by best art in't. Life of my joys,
There were good stuff: I will not trust her with him.
I'll call him back again: he must not keep
Out of my sight so long; I shall grow mad then.

[Enter **DUCHESS**.

DUCHESS [Aside]
He lives not now to see tomorrow spent
If this means take effect, as there's no hardness in't.
Last night he play'd his horrid game again,
Came to my bedside at the full of midnight,
And in his hand that fatal, fearful cup;
Wak'd me, and forc'd me pledge him, to my trembling
And my dead father's scorn; that wounds my sight
That his remembrance should be rais'd in spite.
But either his confusion or mine ends it.—
Oh, Amoretta, hast thou met him yet?
Speak, wench: hast done that for me?

AMORETTA
What, good madam?

DUCHESS
Destruction of my hopes; dost ask that now?
Didst thou not swear to me, out of thy hate
To Almachildes, thou'dst dissemble him
A loving entertainment and a meeting
Where I should work my will?

AMORETTA
Good madam, pardon me:
A loving entertainment I do protest
Myself to give him, with all speed I can, too,

But as I'm yet a maid, a perfect one
As the old time was wont to afford, when
There was few tricks and little cunning stirring,
I can dissemble none that will serve your turn.
He must have ev'n a right one, and a plain one.

DUCHESS
Thou makst me doubt thy health: speak, art thou well?

AMORETTA
Oh, never better. If he would make haste
And come back quickly: he stays now too long.

DUCHESS [Aside]
I'm quite lost in this woman.

[The ribbon falls from **AMORETTA'S** bosom.

What's that fell
Out of her bosom now? Some love token.

AMORETTA
Nay, I'll say that for him: he's the uncivilest gentleman,
And every way desertless.

DUCHESS [Aside]
Who's that now
She discommends so fast?

AMORETTA
I could not love him, madam,
Of any man in court.

DUCHESS
What's he now, prithee?

AMORETTA
Who should it be but Almachildes, madam?
I never hated man so deeply yet.

DUCHESS
As Almachildes?

AMORETTA
I am sick, good madam,
When I but hear him named.

DUCHESS

How is this possible?
But now thou saidst thou lov'dst him, and didst raise him
'Bove all the court in praises.

AMORETTA
How great people
May speak their pleasure, madam; but surely I
Should think the worse of my tongue while I liv'd then.

DUCHESS
No longer have I patience to forbear thee,
Thou that retain'st an envious soul to goodness.
He is a gentleman deserves as much
As ever fortune yet bestow'd on man,
The glory and prime lustre of our court,
Nor can there any but ourself be worthy of him;
And take you notice of that now from me,
Say you have warning on't: if you did love him,
You must not now.

AMORETTA
Let your grace never fear it.

DUCHESS
Thy name is Amoretta, as ours is,
'T has made me love and trust thee.

AMORETTA
And my faithfulness
Has appeared well i' th' proof still, has't not, madam?

DUCHESS
But if't fail now, 'tis nothing.

AMORETTA
Then it shall not.
I know he will not be long from flutt'ring
About this place now h'as had a sight of me,
And I'll perform
In all that I vow'd, madam, faithfully.

DUCHESS
Then am I bless'd, both in revenge and love,
And thou shalt taste the sweetness.

[Exit. Enter **ALMACHILDES**.

AMORETTA [Aside]

What your aims be
I list not to enquire: all I desire
Is to preserve a computent honesty
Both for mine own and his use that shall have me,
Whose luck soe'er it be. Oh, he's return'd already;
I knew he would not fail.

ALMACHILDES [Aside]
It works by this time
Or the devil's in't, I think: I'll never trust witch else
Nor sup with 'em this twelvemonth.

AMORETTA [Aside]
I must soothe him now,
And 'tis great pain to do't against one's stomach.

ALMACHILDES
Now, Amoretta?

AMORETTA
Now y'are well come, sir,
If you'ld come always thus.

ALMACHILDES
Oh, am I so?
Is the case alter'd since?

AMORETTA
If you'ld be rul'd
And know your times, 'twere somewhat a great comfort.
'Las, I could be as loving and as venturous
As any woman (we're all flesh and blood, man)
If you could play the game out modestly
And not betray your hand. I must have care, sir.
You know I have a marriage-time to come,
And that's for life: your best folks will be merry,
But look to the main chance, that's reputation,
And then do what they list.

ALMACHILDES
Wilt hear my oath?
By the sweet health of youth, I will be careful
And never prate on't, nor like a cunning snarer
Make thy clipp'd name the bird to call in others.

AMORETTA
Well, yielding then to such conditions
As my poor bashfulness shall require from you,

I shall yield shortly after.

ALMACHILDES
I'll consent to 'em,
And may thy sweet humility be a pattern
For all proud women living.

AMORETTA
They're beholding to you.

[Exeunt.

SCENE III - A Farmhouse

Enter **ABBERZANES** and an Old Woman with a **BABY**.

ABBERZANES
So, so, away with him: I love to get 'em,
But not to keep 'em. Dost thou know the house?

OLD WOMAN
No matter for the house, I know the porch.

ABBERZANES
There's sixpence more for that; away, keep close.

[Gives her money, then she exits.

My tailor told me he sent away a maid-servant
Well ballast of all sides within these nine days;
His wife nev'r dream'd on't: gave the drab ten pound,
And she nev'r troubles him. A common fashion
He told me 'twas to rid away a 'scape,
And I have sent him this for't. I remember
A friend of mine once serv'd a prating tradesman
Just on this fashion, to a hair, in troth.
'Tis a good ease to a man; you can swell a maid up
And rid her for ten pound: there's the purse back again
Whate'er becomes of your money or your maid.
This comes of bragging now. It's well for the boy, too:
He'll get an excellent trade by't, and on Sundays
Go like a gentleman that has pawn'd his rapier.
He need not care what countryman his father was
Nor what his mother was when he was gotten.
The boy will do well, certain: give him grace
To have a quick hand and convey things cleanly,

'Twill be his own another day.

[Enter **FRANCISCA**.

O, well said!
Art almost furnish'd? There's such a toil always
To set a woman to horse, a mighty trouble.
The letter came to your brother's hand I know
On Thursday last by noon; you were expected there
Yesterday night.

FRANCISCA
It makes the better, sir.

ABBERZANES
We must take heed we ride through all the puddles
'Twixt this and that now, that your safeguard there
May be most probably dabbled.

FRANCISCA
Alas, sir,
I never mark'd till now: I hate myself,
How monstrous thin I look!

ABBERZANES
Not monstrous, neither:
A little sharp i' th' nose, like a country woodcock.

FRANCISCA
Fie, fie, how pale I am! I shall betray myself.
I would you'ld box me well, and handsomely,
To get me into colour.

ABBERZANES
Not I, pardon me:
That let a husband do when he has married you;
A friend at court will never offer that.
Come, how much spice and sugar have you left now
At this poor one month's voyage?

FRANCISCA
Sure, not much, sir.
I think some quarter of a pound of sugar
And half an ounce of spice.

ABBERZANES
Here's no sweet charge!
And there was thirty pound, good weight and true,

Beside what my man stole when 'twas a-weighing,
And that was three pound more, I'll speak with least.
The Rhenish wine, is't all run out in caudles, too?

FRANCISCA
Do you ask that, sir? 'Tis of a week's departure.
You see what 'tis now to get children, sir.

[Enter **BOY**.

BOY
Your mares are ready both, sir.

ABBERZANES
Come, we'll up, then.
Youth, give my sister a straight wand; there's twopence.

BOY
I'll give her a fine whip, sir.

ABBERZANES
No, no, no,
Though we have both deserv'd it.

BOY
Here's a new one.

ABBERZANES
Prithee talk to us of no whips, good boy;
My heart aches when I see 'em. Let's away.

[Exeunt.

ACT III

SCENE I - The Duke's Palace

Enter **DUCHESS**, leading **ALMACHILDES** blindfold.

ALMACHILDES
This you that was a maid, how are you born
To deceive men! I had thought to have married you:
I had been finely handled, had I not?
I'll say that man is wise ever hereafter
That tries his wife beforehand: 'tis no marvel
You should profess such bashfulness to blind one,

As if you durst not look a man i' th' face,
Your modesty would blush so. Why do you not run
And tell the Duchess now? Go, you should tell all;
Let her know this, too. [Aside] Why, here's the plague now:
'Tis hard at first to win 'em; when they're gotten,
There's no way to be rid on 'em, they stick
To a man like bird-lime.—My oath's out:
Will you release me? I'll release myself else.

DUCHESS
Nay, sure I'll bring you to your sights again.

[Takes off his blindfold.

Say, thou must either die or kill the Duke,
For one of them thou must do.

ALMACHILDES
How, good madam?

DUCHESS
Thou hast thy choice, and to that purpose, sir,
I've given thee knowledge of what thou hast,
And what thou must do to be worthy on't.
You must not think to come by such a fortune
Without desert; that were unreasonable.
He that's not born to honour must not look
To have it come with ease to him; he must win't.
Take but unto thine actions wit and courage;
That's all we ask of thee: but if through weakness
Of a poor spirit thou deniest me this,
Think but how thou shalt die, as I'll work means for't,
No murderer ever like thee; for I purpose
To call this subtle, sinful snare of mine
An act of force from thee. Thou'rt proud and youthful,
I shall be believ'd; besides, thy wantonness
Is at this hour in question 'mongst our women,
Which will make ill for thee.

ALMACHILDES
I had hard chance
To light upon this pleasure that's so costly:
'Tis not content with what a man can do
And give him breath, but seeks to have that, too.

DUCHESS
Well, take thy choice.

ALMACHILDES
I see no choice in't, madam,
For 'tis all death, methinks.

DUCHESS
Thou'st an ill sight then
Of a young man; 'tis death if thou refuse it,
And say my zeal has warn'd thee: but consenting,
'Twill be new life, great honour, and my love,
Which in perpetual bands I'll fasten to thee.

ALMACHILDES
How, madam?

DUCHESS
I'll do't religiously,
Make thee my husband: may I lose all sense
Of pleasure in life else, and be more miserable
Than ever creature was, for nothing lives
But has a joy in somewhat.

ALMACHILDES
Then by all
The hopeful fortunes of a young man's rising,
I will perform it, madam.

DUCHESS [Kisses him.]
There's a pledge then
Of a duchess' love for thee. And now trust me
For thy most happy safety: I will choose
That time shall never hurt thee; when a man
Shows resolution, and there's worth in him,
I'll have a care of him. Part now for this time,
But still be near about us till thou canst
Be nearer, that's ourself.

ALMACHILDES
And that I'll venture hard for.

DUCHESS
Good speed to thee.

[Exeunt.

SCENE II - The Grounds of Antonio's House

Enter **GASPERO** and **FLORIDA**.

FLORIDA
Prithee be careful of me, very careful now.

GASPERO
I warrant you, he that cannot be careful of a quean can be careful of nobody: 'tis every man's humour, that. I should nev'r look to a wife half so handsomely.

FLORIDA
Oh softly, sweet sir; should your mistress meet me now in her own house, I were undone forever.

GASPERO
Never fear her, she's at her pricksong close;
There's all the joy she has or takes delight in.
Look, here's the garden key, my master gave't me,
And will'd me to be careful: doubt not you on't.

FLORIDA
Your master is a noble complete gentleman,
And does a woman all the right that may be.

[Enter **SEBASTIAN** disguised. Exit **FLORIDA**.

SEBASTIAN
How now? What's she?

GASPERO
A kind of doubtful creature;
I'll tell thee more anon.

[Exit **GASPERO**.

SEBASTIAN
I know that face
To be a strumpet's, or mine eye is envious
And would fain wish it so where I would have it.
I fail if the condition of this fellow
Wears not about it a strong scent of baseness.
I saw her once before here; five days since 'tis,
And the same wary panderous diligence
Was then bestow'd on her. She came alter'd then,
And more inclining to the city tuck.
Whom should this piece of transformation visit
After the common courtesy of frailty
In our house here? Surely not any servant;
They are not kept so lusty, she so low.
I'm at a strange stand.

[Enter **GASPERO**.

Love and luck assist me!
The truth I shall win from him by false play;
He's now returned.—Well, sir, as you were saying,
Go forward with your tale.

GASPERO
What? I know nothing.

SEBASTIAN
The gentlewoman.

GASPERO
She's gone out at back door now.

SEBASTIAN
Then farewell she, and you, if that be all.

GASPERO
Come, come, thou shalt have more: I have no power
To lock myself up from thee.

SEBASTIAN
So methinks.

GASPERO
You shall not think; trust me, sir, you shall not.
Your ear: she's one o' th' falling family,
A quean my master keeps; she lies at Rutney's.

SEBASTIAN
Is't possible? I thought I had seen her somewhere.

GASPERO
I tell you truth sincerely. Sh'as been thrice here
By stealth within these ten days, and departed still
With pleasure and with thanks, sir; 'tis her luck.
Surely I think if ever there were man
Bewitch'd in this world, 'tis my master, sirrah.

SEBASTIAN
Thinkest thou so, Gasper?

GASPERO
Oh, sir, too apparent.

SEBASTIAN [Aside]
This may prove happy: 'tis the likeliest means
That fortune yet e'er show'd me.

[Enter **ISABELLA**.

ISABELLA
You're both here now,
And strangers newly lighted: where's your attendance?

SEBASTIAN [Aside]
I know what makes you waspish: a pox on't,
She'll every day be angry now at nothing.

[Exeunt **SEBASTIAN** and **GASPERO**.

ISABELLA
I'll call her stranger ever in my heart;
Sh'as kill'd the name of sister through base lust
And fled to shifts. Oh, how a brother's good thoughts
May be beguil'd in woman! Here's a letter,
Found in her absence, reports strangely of her
And speaks her impudence: sh'as undone herself—
I could not hold from weeping when I read it—
Abus'd her brother's house and his good confidence.
'Twas done not like herself: I blame her much.
But if she can but keep it from his knowledge,
I will not grieve him first; it shall not come
By my means to his heart.

[Enter **GASPERO**.

Now, sir, the news?

GASPERO
You call'd 'em strangers: 'tis my master's sister, madam.

ISABELLA
Oh, is't so? She's welcome. Who's come with her?

GASPERO
I see none but Abberzanes.

[Exit.

ISABELLA
He's enough
To bring a woman to confusion,

More than a wiser man, or a far greater.
A letter came last week to her brother's hands
To make way for her coming up again,
After her shame was lighten'd; and she writ there
The gentleman her mother wish'd her to,
Taking a violent surfeit at a wedding,
Died ere she came to see him: what strange cunning
Sin helps a woman to! Here she comes now.

[Enter **ABBERZANES** and **FRANCISCA**.

Sister, you're welcome home again.

FRANCISCA
Thanks, sweet sister.

ISABELLA
Y'have had good speed.

FRANCISCA [Aside]
What says she?—I have made
All the best speed I could.

ISABELLA
I well believe you.
Sir, we're all much beholding to your kindness.

ABBERZANES
My services ever, madam, to a gentlewoman.
I took a bonny mare I keep and met her
Some ten mile out of town: eleven, I think.
'Twas at the stump I met you, I remember,
At bottom of the hill.

FRANCISCA
'Twas there about, sir.

ABBERZANES
Full eleven then, by the rod, if they were measur'd.

ISABELLA
You look ill, methinks; have you been sick of late?
Troth, very bleak, does she not? How think you, sir?

ABBERZANES
No, no: a little sharp with riding; sh'as rid sore.

FRANCISCA

I ever look lean after a journey, sister;
One shall do that has travell'd, travell'd hard.

ABBERZANES
Till evening I commend you to yourselves, ladies.

[Exit.

ISABELLA [Aside]
And that's best trusting, too, if you were hang'd.—
Y'are well acquainted with his hand went out now?

FRANCISCA
His hand?

ISABELLA
I speak of nothing else; I think 'tis there.

[Hands her a letter, which she reads.

Please you to look upon't: and when y'have done
If you did weep, it could not be amiss,
A sign you could say grace after a full meal.
You had not need look paler; yet you do:
'Twas ill done to abuse yourself and us,
To wrong so good a brother, and the thoughts
That we both held of you. I did doubt you much
Before our marriage-day: but then my strangeness
And better hope still kept me off from speaking.
Yet may you find a kind and peaceful sister of me
If you desist here and shake hands with folly,
Which you ha' more cause to do than I to wish you;
As truly as I bear a love to goodness,
Your brother knows not yet on't, nor shall ever
For my part, so you leave his company:
But if I find you impudent in sinning,
I will not keep't an hour; nay, prove your enemy
And you know who will aid me. As y'have goodness,
You may make use of this; I'll leave it with you.

[Exit.

FRANCISCA
Here's a sweet churching after a woman's labour,
And a fine "Give you joy!" Why, where the devil
Lay you to be found out? The sudden hurry
Of hast'ning to prevent shame brought shame forth.
That's still the curse of all lascivious stuff;

Misdeeds could never yet be wary enough.
Now must I stand in fear of every look,
Nay, tremble at a whisper: she can keep it secret?
That's very likely, and a woman, too!
I'm sure I could not do't: and I am made
As well as she can be for any purpose.
'Twould never stay with me two days: I have cast it;
The third would be a terrible sick-day with me,
Not possible to bear it. Should I then
Trust to her strength in't, that lies every night
Whispering the daily news in a husband's ear?
No, and I have thought upon the means: bless'd fortune,
I must be quit with her in the same fashion,
Or else 'tis nothing; there's no way like it
To bring her honesty into question cunningly.
My brother will believe small likelihoods
Coming from me, too; I, lying now i' th' house,
May work things to my will beyond conceit, too.
Disgrace her first, her tale will nev'r be heard:
I learn'd that counsel first of a sound guard.
I do suspect Gasper, my brother's squire there,
Had some hand in this mischief, for he's cunning,
And I perhaps may fit him.

[Enter **ANTONIO**.

ANTONIO
Your sister told me
You were come: thou'rt welcome.

FRANCISCA
Where is she?

ANTONIO
Who? My wife?

FRANCISCA
Ay, sir.

ANTONIO
Within.

FRANCISCA
Not within hearing, think you?

ANTONIO
Within hearing?
What's thy conceit in that? Why shak'st thy head so?

And look'st so pale and poorly?

FRANCISCA
I'm a fool indeed
To take such grief for others, for your fortune, sir.

ANTONIO
My fortune? [Aside] Worse things yet? Farewell life then!

FRANCISCA
I fear y'are much deceiv'd, sir, in this woman.

ANTONIO
Who? In my wife? Speak low: come hither, softly, sister.

FRANCISCA
I love her as a woman you made choice of,
But when she wrongs you, natural love is touch'd, brother,
And that will speak, you know.

ANTONIO
I trust it will.

FRANCISCA
I held a shrewd suspicion of her lightness
At first when I went down, which made me haste the sooner.
But more, to make amends, at my return now
I found apparent signs.

ANTONIO
Apparent, say'st thou?

FRANCISCA
Ay, and of base lust, too; that makes th' affliction.

ANTONIO
There has been villainy wrought upon me then,
'Tis too plain now.

FRANCISCA
Happy are they, I say still,
That have their sisters living i' th' house with 'em,
Their mothers, or some kindred: a great comfort
To all poor married men; it is not possible
A young wife can abuse a husband then,
'Tis found straight. But swear secrecy to this, brother.

ANTONIO

To this, and all thou wilt have.

FRANCISCA
Then this follows, sir.

[She whispers to him.

ANTONIO
I praise thy counsel well: I'll put 't in use straight.

[Exit **FRANCISCA**. Enter **ISABELLA**.

[Aside] See where she comes herself.—Kind, honest lady,
I must borrow a whole forthnight's leave of thee.

ISABELLA
How, sir? A forthnight's?

ANTONIO
It may be but ten days; I know not yet.
'Tis business for the state, and 't must be done.

ISABELLA
I wish good speed to't then.

ANTONIO
Why, that was well spoke.
I'll take but a footboy: I need no more.
The rest I'll leave at home to do you service.

ISABELLA
Use your own pleasure, sir.

ANTONIO
'Till my return
You'll be good company, my sister and you?

ISABELLA
We shall make shift, sir.

ANTONIO
I'm glad now she's come,
And so the wishes of my love to both.

[Exit.

ISABELLA
And our good prayers with you, sir.

[Enter **SEBASTIAN** disguised.

SEBASTIAN [Aside]
Now my fortune!—
By your kind favour, madam.

ISABELLA
With me, sir?

SEBASTIAN
The words shall not be many, but the faithfulness
And true respect that is included in 'em
Is worthy your attention, and may put upon me
The fair repute of a just, honest servant.

ISABELLA
What's here to do, sir,
There's such great preparation toward?

SEBASTIAN
In brief, that goodness in you is abus'd, madam;
You have the married life, but 'tis a strumpet
That has the joy on't, and the fruitfulness:
There goes away your comfort.

ISABELLA
How? A strumpet?

SEBASTIAN
Of five years' cost and upwards, a dear mischief,
As they are all of 'em; his forthnight's journey
Is to that country, if it be not rudeness
To speak the truth: I have found it all out, madam.

ISABELLA
Thou'st found out thine own ruin, for to my knowledge
Thou does belie him basely: I dare swear
He's a gentleman, as free from that folly
As ever took religious life upon him.

SEBASTIAN
Be not too confident to your own abuse, madam.
Since I have begun the truth, neither your frowns—
The only curses that I have on earth
Because my means depend upon your service—
Nor all the execration of man's fury
Shall put me off: though I be poor, I'm honest

And too just in this business. I perceive now
Too much respect and faithfulness to ladies
May be a wrong to servants.

ISABELLA
Art thou yet
So impudent to stand in't?

SEBASTIAN
Are you yet so cold, madam,
In the belief on't? There my wonder's fix'd,
Having such blessed health and youth about you,
Which makes the injury mighty.

ISABELLA
Why, I tell thee
It were too great a fortune for thy lowness
To find out such a thing: thou does not look
As if thou'rt made for't. By the precious sweets of love,
I would give half my wealth for such a bargain
And think 'twere bought too cheap: thou canst not guess
Thy means and happiness should I find this true.
First, I'ld prefer thee to the lord my uncle,
He's Governor of Ravenna; all the advancements
I' th' kingdom flow from him: what need I boast that
Which common fame can teach thee?

SEBASTIAN
Then thus, madam:
Since I presume now on your height of spirit
And your regard to your own youth and fruitfulness,
Which every woman naturally loves and covets,
Accept but of my labour in directions.
You shall both find your wrongs, which you may right
At your own pleasure, yet not miss'd tonight
Here in the house neither: none shall take notice
Of any absence in you, as I have thought on't.

ISABELLA
Do this, and take my praise and thanks forever.

SEBASTIAN
As I deserve, I wish 'em, and will serve you.

[Exeunt.

Enter **HECATE, STADLIN, HOPPO, PUCKLE** and other **WITCHES**, and **FIRESTONE**.

HECATE
The moon's a gallant, see how brisk she rides.

STADLIN
Here's a rich evening, Hecate.

HECATE
Ay, is't not, wenches,
To take a journey of five thousand mile?

HOPPO
Ours will be more tonight.

HECATE
Oh, 'twill be precious:
Heard you the owl yet?

STADLIN
Briefly in the copse,
As we came through now.

HECATE
'Tis high time for us then.

STADLIN
There was a bat hung at my lips three times
As we came through the woods and drank her fill.
Old Puckle saw her.

HECATE
You are fortunate still;
The very shriek-owl lights upon your shoulder
And woos you like a pigeon. Are you furnish'd?
Have you your ointments?

STADLIN
All.

HECATE
Prepare to flight then.
I'll overtake you swiftly.

STADLIN
Hie thee, Hecate:

We shall be up betimes.

HECATE
I'll reach you quickly.

[Exeunt all but **HECATE** and **FIRESTONE**.

FIRESTONE [Aside]
They're all going a-birding tonight: they talk of fowls i' th' air that fly by day; I am sure they'll be a company of foul sluts there tonight: if we have not mortality after it, I'll be hang'd, for they are able to putrefy it, to infect a whole region.
She spies me now.

HECATE
What, Firestone , our sweet son?

FIRESTONE [Aside]
A little sweeter than some of you, or a dunghill were too good for me.

HECATE
How much hast here?

FIRESTONE
Nineteen, and all brave plump ones,
Besides six lizards and three serpentine eggs.

HECATE
Dear and sweet boy! What herbs hast thou?

FIRESTONE
I have some mar-martin and mandragon.

HECATE
Marmaritin and mandragora, thou wouldst say.
Here's panax, too: I thank thee.

FIRESTONE
My pan aches, I am sure,
With kneeling down to cut 'em.

HECATE
And selago,
Hedge-hyssop, too: how near he goes my cuttings!
Were they all cropp'd by moonlight?

FIRESTONE
Every blade of 'em,
Or I am a mooncalf, mother.

HECATE
Hie thee home with 'em.
Look well to the house tonight; I am for aloft.

FIRESTONE [Aside]
Aloft, quoth you? I would you would break your neck once,
That I might have all quickly.—Hark, hark, mother.
They are above the steeple already, flying
Over your head with a noise of musicians.

HECATE
They are they indeed. Help, help me: I'm too late else.

Song, [the witches in the air offstage].

WITCHES
Come away, come away,
Hecate, Hecate, come away.

HECATE
I come, I come, I come, I come,
With all the speed I may,
With all the speed I may,
Where's Stadlin?

STADLIN
Here.

HECATE
Where's Puckle?

PUCKLE
Here.

WITCHES
And Hoppo, too, and Hellwain, too;
We lack but you, we lack but you.
Come away, make up the count.

HECATE
I will but 'noint, and then I mount.
A spirit like a cat descends.

WITCHES
There's one comes down to fetch his dues,
A kiss, a coll, a sip of blood,
And why thou stay'st so long

I muse, I muse,
Since the air's so sweet and good.

HECATE
Oh, art thou come?
What news, what news?

MALKIN
All goes still to our delight,
Either come or else
Refuse, refuse.

HECATE
Now I am furnish'd for the flight.

FIRESTONE
Hark, hark, the cat sings a brave treble in her own language!

HECATE [going up]
Now I go, now I fly,
Malkin my sweet spirit and I.
Oh, what a dainty pleasure 'tis
To ride in the air
When the moon shines fair
And sing, and dance, and toy, and kiss;
Over woods, high rocks, and mountains,
Over seas, over misty fountains,
Over steeples, towers, and turrets,
We fly by night, 'mongst troops of spirits.
No ring of bells to our ears sounds,
No howls of wolves, no yelps of hounds,
No, not the noise of water's breach
Or cannon's throat our height can reach.
No ring of bells, etc.

[**HECATE** and her spirit ascend out of view.

FIRESTONE
Well, mother, I thank your kindness. You must be gambolling i' th' air and leave me to walk here like a fool and a mortal.

[Exit.

ACT IV

SCENE I - The Duke's Palace

Enter **ALMACHILDES**.

ALMACHILDES
Though the fates have endued me with a pretty kind of lightness that I can laugh at the world in a corner on't, and can make myself merry on fasting-nights to rub out a supper (which were a precious quality in a young, formal studient), yet let the world know there is some difference betwixt my jovial condition and the lunary state of madness. I am not quite out of my wits: I know a bawd from an aqua vite shop, a strumpet from wildfire, and a beadle from brimstone. Now shall I try the honesty of a great woman soundly; she reck'ning the duke's made away, I'll be hang'd if I be not the next now. If I trust her, as she's a woman, let one of her long hairs wind about my heart and be the end of me, which were a piteous, lamentable tragedy, and might be entitled A Fair Warning for All Hair Bracelets.
Already there's an insurrection
Among the people; they are up in arms
Not out of any reason, but their wills,
Which are in them their saints, sweating and swearing
Out of their zeal to rudeness that no stranger,
As they term her, shall govern over them,
They say they'll raise a Duke among themselves first.

[Enter **DUCHESS**.

DUCHESS
Oh, Almachildes, I perceive already
Our loves are born to crosses! We're beset
By multitudes, and which is worse, I fear me
Unfriended too of any. My chief care
Is for thy sweet youth's safety.

ALMACHILDES [Aside]
He that believes you not
Goes the right way to heaven, o' my conscience.

DUCHESS
There is no trusting of 'em: they are all as barren
In pity as in faith. He that puts confidence
In them dies openly to the sight of all men,
Not with his friends and neighbours in peace private,
But as his shame, so his cold farewell is,
Public and full of noise. But keep you close, sir,
Not seen of any till I see the way
Plain for your safety. I expect the coming
Of the lord Governor, whom I will flatter
With fair entreaties to appease their wildness,
And before him take a great grief upon me
For the duke's death, his strange and sudden loss;
And when a quiet comes, expect thy joys.

ALMACHILDES [Aside]
I do expect now to be made away
'Twixt this and Tuesday night; if I live Wednesday,
Say I have been careful and shunn'd spoon-meat.

[Exit.

DUCHESS
This fellow lives too long after the deed;
I'm weary of his sight: he must die quickly
Or I've small hope of safety. My great aim's
At the lord governor's love; he is a spirit
Can sway and countenance: these obey and crouch.
My guiltiness had need of such a master
That with a beck can suppress multitudes
And dim misdeeds with radiance of his glory
Not to be seen with dazzled popular eyes.

[Enter Lord **GOVERNOR**.

And here behold him come.

GOVERNOR [To one within]
Return back to 'em;
Say we desire 'em to be friends of peace
Till they hear farther from us.

DUCHESS
O my lord,
I fly unto the pity of your nobleness,
The grieved'st lady that was e'er beset
With storms of sorrows or wild rage of people!
Never was woman's grief for loss of lord
Dearer than mine to me.

GOVERNOR
There's no right done
To him now, madam, by wrong done to yourself;
Your own good wisdom may instruct you so far:
And for the people's tumult, which oft grows
From liberty or rankness of long peace,
I'll labour to restrain, as I've begun, madam.

DUCHESS
My thanks and prayers shall nev'r forget you, sir,
And, in time to come, my love.

GOVERNOR

Your love, sweet madam?
You make my joys too happy: I did covet
To be the fortunate man that blessing visits,
Which I'll esteem the crown and full reward
Of service present, and deserts to come.
It is a happiness I'll be bold to sue for
When I have set a calm upon these spirits
That now are up for ruin.

DUCHESS
Sir, my wishes
Are so well met in yours, so fairly answer'd
And nobly recompens'd, it makes me suffer
In those extremes that few have ever felt,
To hold two passions in one heart at once,
Of gladness and of sorrow.

GOVERNOR
Then as the olive
Is the meek ensign of fair fruitful peace,
So is this kiss of yours.

DUCHESS
Love's power be with you, sir.

GOVERNOR [Aside]
How sh'as betray'd her! May I breathe no longer
Than to do virtue service and bring forth
The fruits of noble thoughts, honest and loyal!
This will be worth th' observing; and I'll do it.

[Exit.

DUCHESS
What a sure happiness confirms joy to me,
Now in the times of my most imminent dangers!
I look'd for ruin, and increase of honour
Meets me auspiciously. But my hopes are clogg'd now
With an unworthy weight: there's the misfortune.
What course shall I take now with this young man?
For he must be no hindrance. I have thought on't.
I'll take some witch's counsel for his end,
That will be sur'st. Mischief is mischief's friend.

[Exit.

Enter **SEBASTIAN** disguised and **FERNANDO**.

SEBASTIAN
If ever you knew force of love in life, sir,
Give to mine pity.

FERNANDO
You do ill to doubt me.

SEBASTIAN
I could make bold with no friend seemlier
Than with yourself because you were in presence
At our vow-making.

FERNANDO
I am a witness to't.

SEBASTIAN
Then you best understand of all men living
This is no wrong I offer, no abuse
Either to faith or friendship, for we are register'd
Husband and wife in heaven; though there wants that
Which often keeps licentious men in awe
From starting from their wedlocks, the knot public.
'Tis in our souls knit fast, and how more precious
The soul is than the body, so much judge
The sacred and celestial tie within us
More than the outward form, which calls but witness
Here upon earth to what is done in heaven,
Though I must needs confess, the least is honourable,
As an ambassador sent from a king
Has honour by the employment, yet there's greater
Dwells in the king that sent him; so in this.

[Enter **FLORIDA**.

FERNANDO
I approve all you speak, and will appear to you
A faithful, pitying friend.

SEBASTIAN
Look, there is she, sir,
One good for nothing but to make use of,
And I'm constrained to employ her to make all things
Plain, easy, and probable; for when she comes
And finds one here that claims him, as I have taught

Both this to do't and he to compound with her,
'Twill stir belief the more of such a business.

FERNANDO
I praise the carriage well.

SEBASTIAN
Hark you, sweet mistress,
I shall do you a simple turn in this:
For she disgrac'd thus, you are up in favour
Forever with her husband.

FLORIDA
That's my hope, sir;
I would not take the pains else. Have you the keys
Of the garden-side that I may get betimes in
Closely, and take her lodging?

SEBASTIAN
Yes, I have thought upon you;
Here be the keys.

[He gives her the keys.

FLORIDA
Marry, and thanks, sweet sir;
Set me a-work so still.

SEBASTIAN [Aside]
Your joys are false ones:
You're like to lie alone; you'll be deceiv'd
Of the bedfellow you look for, else my purpose
Were in an ill case. He's on his forthnight's journey.
You'll find cold comfort there: a dream will be
Even the best market you can make tonight.—
She'll not be long now; you may lose no time neither:
If she but take you at the door, 'tis enough.
When a suspect doth catch once, it burns mainly.
There may you end your business, and as cunningly
As if you were i' th' chamber, if you please,
To use but the same art.

FLORIDA
What need you urge that
Which comes so naturally I cannot miss on't?
What makes the devil so greedy of a soul
But 'cause h'as lost his own, to all joys lost?
So 'tis our trade to set snares for other women

'Cause we were once caught ourselves.

[Exit.

SEBASTIAN
A sweet allusion!
Hell and a whore it seems are partners then
In one ambition. Yet thou'rt here deceiv'd now;
Thou canst set none to hurt, or wrong her honour:
It rather makes it perfect. Best of friends
That ever love's extremities were bless'd with,
I feel mine arms with thee, and call my peace
The offspring of thy friendship. I will think
This night my wedding night, and with a joy
As reverend, as religion can make man's,
I will embrace this blessing: honest actions
Are laws unto themselves, and that good fear
Which is on others forc'd grows kindly there.

[Knocking within.

FERNANDO
Hark, hark! One knocks; away, sir, 'tis she certainly.
It sounds much like a woman's jealous 'larum.

[Exit **SEBASTIAN**. Enter **ISABELLA**.

ISABELLA
By your leave, sir.

FERNANDO
Y'are welcome, gentlewoman.

ISABELLA [Aside]
Our ladyship, then, stands us in no stead now.—
One word in private, sir. [Whispers to him.]

FERNANDO
No, surely, forsooth,
There is no such here, y'have mistook the house.

ISABELLA
Oh, sir, that have I not: excuse me there,
I come not with such ignorance. Think not so, sir.
'Twas told me at the ent'ring of your house here
By one that knows him too well.

FERNANDO

Who should that be?

ISABELLA
Nay, sir, betraying is not my profession.
But here I know he is, and I presume
He would give me admittance, if he knew on't,
As one on's nearest friends.

FERNANDO
Y'are not his wife, forsooth?

ISABELLA
Yes, by my faith, am I.

FERNANDO
Cry you mercy then, lady.

ISABELLA [Aside]
She goes here by the name on's wife: good stuff!
But the bold strumpet never told me that.

FERNANDO
We are so oft deceiv'd that let out lodgings,
We know not whom to trust: 'tis such a world,
There are so many odd tricks now-a-days
Put upon housekeepers.

ISABELLA
Why? Do you think I'ld wrong
You or the reputation of your house?
Pray show me the way to him.

FERNANDO
He's asleep, lady,
The curtains drawn about him.

ISABELLA
Well, well, sir,
I'll have that care, I'll not disease him much.
Tread you but lightly. [Aside] Oh, of what gross falsehood
Is man's heart made of! Had my first love liv'd
And return'd safe, he would have been a light
To all men's actions, his faith shin'd so bright.

[Exeunt. Enter **SEBASTIAN** disguised.

SEBASTIAN
I cannot so deceive her, 'twere too sinful;

There's more religion in my love than so.
It is not treacherous lust that gives content
T'an honest mind: and this could prove no better.
Were it in me a part of manly justice,
That have sought strange, hard means to keep her chaste
To her first vow, and I t'abuse her first?
Better I never knew what comfort were
In woman's love than wickedly to know it.
What could the falsehood of one night avail him
That must enjoy forever, or he's lost?
'Tis the way rather to draw hate upon me,
For, known, 'tis as impossible she should love me,
As youth in health to dote upon a grief,
Or one that's robb'd and bound t'affect the thief.
No, he that would soul's sacred comfort win
Must burn in pure love like a seraphin.

[Enter **ISABELLA**.

ISABELLA
Celio?

SEBASTIAN
Sweet madam.

ISABELLA
Thou hast deluded me:
There's nobody.

SEBASTIAN
How? I wonder he would miss, madam,
Having appointed, too; 'twere a strange goodness
If heaven should turn his heart now by the way.

ISABELLA
Oh, never, Celio.

SEBASTIAN
Yes, I ha' known the like.
Man is not at his own disposing, madam;
The bless'd powers have provided the better for him,
Or he were miserable: he may come yet;
'Tis early, madam. If you would be pleas'd
To embrace my counsel, you should see this night over,
Since y'have bestowed these pains.

ISABELLA
I intend so.

SEBASTIAN [Aside]
That strumpet would be found, else she should go.
I curse the time now I did ev'r make use
Of such a plague: sin knows not what it does.

[Exeunt.

SCENE III - Antonio's House

Enter **FRANCISCA**, in her chamber above.

FRANCISCA
'Tis now my brother's time, even much about it;
For though he dissembled a whole forthnight's absence,
He comes again tonight: 'twas so agreed
Before he went. I must bestir my wits now
To catch this sister of mine, and bring her name
To some disgrace first to preserve mine own:
There's profit in that cunning. She cast off
My company betimes tonight by tricks and sleights,
And I was well contented: I am resolv'd
There's no hate lost between us, for I know
She does not love me now but painfully,
Like one that's forc'd to smile upon a grief
To bring some purpose forward, and I'll pay her
In her own mettle. They're now all at rest,
And Gasper there, and all: list, fast asleep.
He cries it hither. I must disease you straight, sir.
For the maid-servants and the girls o' th' house,
I spic'd them lately with a drowsy posset;
They will not hear in haste.

[Noise within.

My brother's come!
Oh, where's this key now for him? Here 'tis, happily.
But I must wake him first. Why, Gasper, Gasper!

GASPERO [Within]
What a pox gasp you for?

FRANCISCA [Aside]
Now I'll throw 't down.

GASPERO [Within]

Who's that call'd me now? Somebody call'd Gasper?

FRANCISCA
Oh, up, as thou'rt an honest fellow, Gasper!

GASPERO [Within]
I shall not rise tonight then. What's the matter?
Who's that? Young mistress?

FRANCISCA
Ay; up, up, sweet Gasper!

[Enter **GASPERO** in his nightshirt.

My sister hath both knock'd and call'd this hour,
And not a maid will stir.

GASPERO
They'll stir enough sometimes.

FRANCISCA
Hark, hark again, Gasper! Oh, run, run, prithee!

GASPERO
Give me leave to clothe myself.

FRANCISCA
Stand'st upon clothing
In an extremity? Hark, hark again!
She may be dead ere thou com'st; oh, in quickly!

[Exit **GASPERO**.

He's gone. He cannot choose but be took now
Or met in his return; that will be enough.

[Enter **ANTONIO**.

Brother? Here, take this light.

ANTONIO
My careful sister!

FRANCISCA
Look first in his own lodging ere you enter.

[Exit **ANTONIO**.

ANTONIO [Within]
Oh, abus'd confidence! Here's nothing of him
But what betrays him more!

FRANCISCA
Then 'tis too true, brother.

ANTONIO [Within]
I'll make base lust a terrible example,
No villainy e'er paid dearer!

FLORIDA [Within]
Help! Hold, sir!

ANTONIO [Within]
I am deaf to all humanity!

FRANCISCA
List, list!
A strange and sudden silence after all;
I trust h'as spoil'd 'em both: too dear a happiness!
Oh, how I tremble between doubts and joys!

[Enter **ANTONIO**.

ANTONIO [Aside]
There perish both, down to the house of falsehood
Where perjurous wedlock weeps! Oh, perjurous woman!
Sh'ad took the innocence of sleep upon her
At my approach and would not see me come,
As if sh'ad lain there like a harmless soul
And never dream'd of mischief. What's all this now?
I feel no ease; the burthen's not yet off
So long as th' abuse sticks in my knowledge.
Oh, 'tis a pain of hell to know one's shame!
Had it been hid and done, it had been done happy,
For he that's ignorant lives long and merry.

FRANCISCA [Aside]
I shall know all now.—Brother?

ANTONIO
Come down quickly,
For I must kill thee, too.

FRANCISCA
Me?

ANTONIO

Stay not long
If thou desir'st to die with little pain.
Make haste, I'ld wish thee, and come willingly;
If I be forc'd to come, I shall be cruel
Above a man to thee.

FRANCISCA

Why, sir, my brother?

ANTONIO

Talk to thy soul if thou wilt talk at all;
To me thou'rt lost forever.

FRANCISCA

This is fearful in you
Beyond all reason, brother; would you thus
Reward me for my care and truth shown to you?

ANTONIO

A curse upon 'em both, and thee for company!
'Tis that too diligent, thankless care of thing
Makes me a murderer, and that ruinous truth
That lights me to the knowledge of my shame.
Hadst thou been secret, then had I been happy
And had a hope, like man, of joys to come.
Now here I stand, a stain to my creation:
And, which is heavier than all torments to me,
The understanding of this base adultery,
And that thou told'st me first, which thou deserv'st
Death worthily for.

FRANCISCA

If that be the worst, hold, sir;
Hold, brother, I can ease your knowledge straight,
By my soul's hopes I can: there's no such thing.

ANTONIO

How?

FRANCISCA

Bless me but with life, I'll tell you all.
Your bed was never wrong'd.

ANTONIO

What? Never wrong'd?

FRANCISCA

I ask but mercy, as I deal with truth now:
'Twas only my deceit, my plot and cunning
To bring disgrace upon her, by that means
To keep mine own hid, which none knew but she.
To speak troth, I had a child by Abberzanes, sir.

ANTONIO
How? Abberzanes?

FRANCISCA
And my mother's letter
Was counterfeited to get time and place
For my delivery.

ANTONIO
Oh, my wrath's redoubled!

FRANCISCA
At my return, she could speak all my folly,
And blam'd me, with good counsel. I, for fear
It should be made known, thus rewarded her,
Wrought you into suspicion without cause,
And at your coming, raised up Gasper suddenly,
Sent him but in before you by a falsehood,
Which to your kindled jealousy I knew
Would add enough. What's now confess'd is true.

ANTONIO
The more I hear, the worse it fares with me.
I ha' kill'd 'em now for nothing: yet the shame
Follows my blood still. Once more, come down.
Look you, my sword goes up. Call Hermio to me;
Let the new man alone: he'll wake too soon
To find his mistress dead and lose a service.

[Exit **FRANCISCA**.

Already the day breaks upon my guilt;
I must be brief and sudden. Hermio!

[Enter **HERMIO**.

HERMIO
Sir?

ANTONIO
Run, knock up Abberzanes speedily;
Say I desire his company this morning

To yonder horse race, tell him. That will fetch him.
Oh, hark you, by the way—

HERMIO
Yes, sir?

[**ANTONIO** whispers to him.

ANTONIO
Use speed now,
Or I will ne'er use thee more. And perhaps
I speak in a right hour. My grief o'erflows;
I must in private go and vent my woes.

[Exeunt.

ACT V

SCENE I - Antonio's House

Enter **ANTONIO** and **ABBERZANES**.

ANTONIO
You are welcome, sir.

ABBERZANES
I think I am worthy on't,
For look you, sir, I come untruss'd, in troth.

ANTONIO
The more's the pity—honester men go to't—
That slaves should 'scape it. What blade have you got there?

ABBERZANES
Nay, I know not that, sir. I am not acquainted greatly with the blade; I am sure 'tis a good scabbard, and that satisfies me.

ANTONIO
'Tis long enough indeed, if that be good.

ABBERZANES
I love to wear a long weapon: 'tis a thing commendable.

ANTONIO
I pray draw it, sir.

ABBERZANES

It is not to be drawn.

ANTONIO

Not to be drawn?

ABBERZANES

I do not care to see't. To tell you troth, sir, 'tis only a holiday thing, to wear by a man's side.

ANTONIO

Draw it, or I'll rip thee down from neck to navel, though there's small glory in't.

ABBERZANES

Are you in earnest, sir?

ANTONIO

I'll tell thee that anon.

ABBERZANES

Why, what's the matter, sir?

ANTONIO

What a base misery is this in life now!
This slave had so much daring courage in him
To act a sin would shame whole generations,
But hath not so much honest strength about him
To draw a sword in way of satisfaction.
This shows thy great guilt that thou darest not fight.

ABBERZANES

Yes, I dare fight, sir, in an honest cause.

ANTONIO

Why, come then, slave! Thou'st made my sister a whore.

ABBERZANES

Prove than an honest cause and I'll be hang'd.

ANTONIO

So many starting-holes? Can I light no way?
Go to, you shall have your wish: all honest play.
Come forth, thou fruitful wickedness, thou seed
Of shame and murder.

[Enter **FRANCISCA**.

Take to thee in wedlock
Baseness and cowardice, a fit match for thee.

Come, sir, along with me.

ABBERZANES
'Las, what to do?
I am too young to take a wife, in troth.

ANTONIO
But old enough to take a strumpet, though.
You'ld fain get all your children beforehand,
And marry when y'have done: that's a strange course, sir.
This woman I bestow on thee: what dost thou say?

ABBERZANES
I would I had such another to bestow on you, sir.

ANTONIO
Uncharitable slave, dog, coward as thou art,
To wish a plague so great as thine to any!

ABBERZANES
To my friend, sir, where I think I may be bold.

ANTONIO
Down, and do't solemnly: contract yourselves
With truth and zeal, or ne'er rise up again!
I will not have her die i' th' state of strumpet,
Though she took pride to live one. Hermio, the wine!

[Enter **HERMIO** with wine.

HERMIO
'Tis here, sir. [Aside] Troth, I wonder at some things,
But I'll keep honest.

ANTONIO
So, here's to you both now,
And to your joys, if't be your luck to find 'em.

[Drinks.

I tell you, you must weep hard, if you do.
Divide it 'twixt you both.

[They drink.]

You shall not need
A strong bill of divorcement after that
If you mislike your bargain. Go, get in now,

Kneel, and pray heartily to get forgiveness
Of those two souls whose bodies thou hast murder'd.

[Exeunt **ABBERZANES** and **FRANCISCA**.

Spread, subtle poison! Now my shame in her
Will die when I die; there's some comfort yet.
I do but think how each man's punishment
Proves still a kind of justice to himself.
I was the man that told this innocent gentlewoman,
Whom I did falsely wed and falsely kill,
That he that was her husband first by contract
Was slain i' th' field, and he's known yet to live.
So did I cruelly beguile her heart,
For which I am well rewarded; so is Gasper
Who, to befriend my love, swore fearful oaths;
He saw the last breath fly from him. I see now
'Tis a thing dreadful t' abuse holy vows
And falls most weighty.

HERMIO
Take comfort, sir;
You're guilty of no death: they're only hurt,
And that not mortally.

ANTONIO
Thou breath'st untruths.

[Enter **GASPERO**.

HERMIO
Speak, Gasper, for me then.

GASPERO
Your unjust rage, sir,
Has hurt me without cause.

ANTONIO
'Tis chang'd to grief for't.
How fares my wife?

GASPERO
No doubt, sir, she fares well,
For she nev'r felt your fury: the poor sinner
That hath this seven year kept herself sound for you,
'Tis your luck to bring her into th' surgeon's hands now.

ANTONIO

Florida!

GASPERO
She. I know no other, sir;
You were nev'r at charge yet, but with one light horse.

ANTONIO
Why, where's your lady? Where's my wife tonight then?

GASPERO
Nay, ask me not, sir; your struck doe within
Tells a strange tale of her.

ANTONIO
This is unsufferable!
Never had man such means to make him mad!
Oh, that the poison would but spare my life
Till I had found her out!

HERMIO
Your wish is granted, sir.
Upon the faithfulness of a pitying servant,
I gave you none at all; my heart was kinder.
Let not conceit abuse you; you're as healthful,
For any drug, as life yet ever found you.

[Enter Lord **GOVERNOR**.

ANTONIO
Why, here's a happiness wipes off mighty sorrows;
The benefit of ever-pleasing service
Bless thy profession! Oh, my worthy lord,
I have an ill bargain; never man had worse!
The woman that unworthy wears your blood
To countenance sin in her: your niece, she's false!

GOVERNOR
False?

ANTONIO
Impudent, adulterous!

GOVERNOR
You're too loud,
And grow too bold, too, with her virtuous meekness.
Who dare accuse her?

[Enter **FLORIDA**.

FLORIDA
Here's one dare and can:
She lies this night with Celio, her own servant,
The place, Fernando's house.

GOVERNOR
Thou dost amaze us.

ANTONIO
Why, here's but lust translated from one baseness
Into another; here I thought to have caught 'em,
But lighted wrong by false intelligence
And made me hurt the innocent. But now
I'll make my revenge dreadfuller than a tempest;
An army should not stop me, or a sea
Divide 'em from my revenge.

[Exit.

GOVERNOR
I'll not speak
To have her spar'd if she be base and guilty.
If otherwise, heaven will not see her wrong'd,
I need not take care for her. Let that woman
Be carefully look'd to, both for health and sureness;
[To **FLORIDA**] It is not that mistaken wound thou wear'st
Shall be thy privilege.

FLORIDA
You cannot torture me
Worse than the surgeon does: so long I care not.

[Exit **FLORIDA** and **GASPERO**.

GOVERNOR
If she be adulterous, I will never trust
Virtues in women; they're but veils for lust.

[Exit.

HERMIO
To what a lasting ruin mischief runs!
I had thought I had well and happily ended all
In keeping back the poison, and new rage now
Spreads a worse venom. My poor lady grieves me;
'Tis strange to me that her sweet-seeming virtues
Should be so meanly overtook with Celio,

A servant: 'tis not possible.

[Enter **ISABELLA** and **SEBASTIAN**, disguised.

ISABELLA
Good morrow, Hermio.
My sister stirring yet?

HERMIO
How? Stirring, forsooth!
Here has been simple stirring. Are you not hurt, madam?
Pray speak, we have a surgeon ready.

ISABELLA
How, a surgeon?

HERMIO
Hath been at work these five hours.

ISABELLA
How he talks!

HERMIO
Did you not meet my master?

ISABELLA
How, your master?
Why, came he home tonight?

HERMIO
Then you know nothing, madam?
Please you but walk in, you shall hear strange business.

ISABELLA [To **SEBASTIAN**]
I am much beholding to your truth now, am I not?
Y'have serv'd me fair: my credit's stain'd forever!

[Exeunt **ISABELLA** and **HERMIO**.

SEBASTIAN
This is the wicked'st fortune that e'er blew.
We're both undone for nothing: there's no way
Flatters recovery now, the thing's so gross.
Her disgrace grieves me more than a life's loss.

[Exit.

Enter **DUCHESS, HECATE, FIRESTONE.**

HECATE
What death is't you desire for Almachildes?

DUCHESS
A sudden and a subtle.

HECATE
Then I have fitted you.
Here lie the gifts of both sudden and subtle:
His picture made in wax and gently molten
By a blue fire kindled with dead men's eyes
Will waste him by degrees.

DUCHESS
In what time, prithee?

HECATE
Perhaps in a moon's progress.

DUCHESS
What? A month?
Out upon pictures, if they be so tedious!
Give me things with some life.

HECATE
Then seek no farther.

DUCHESS
This must be done with speed, dispatch'd this night,
If it may possible.

HECATE
I have if for you.
Here's that will do't: stay but perfection's time,
And that's not five hours hence.

DUCHESS
Canst thou do this?

HECATE
Can I?

DUCHESS

I mean, so closely.

HECATE
So closely
Do you mean, too?

DUCHESS
So artfully, so cunningly.

HECATE
Worse and worse; doubts and incredulities!
They make me mad: let scrupulous greatness know
Cum volui, ripis ipsis mirantibus, amnes
In fontes rediere suos; concussaque, sisto
Stantia, concutio cantu freta; nubila pello
Nubilaque induco; ventos abigoque vocoque;
Vipereas rumpo verbis et carmine fauces;
Et silvas moveo, jubeoque tremiscere montes,
Et mugire solum, manesque exire sepulchris.
Te quoque, luna, traho. Can you doubt me then, daughter,
That can make mountains tremble, miles of woods walk,
Whole earth's foundation bellow, and the spirits
Of the entomb'd to burst out from their marbles,
Nay, draw yond moon to my envolv'd designs?

FIRESTONE [Aside]
I know as well as can be when my mother's mad and our great cat angry, for one spits French then and th'other spits Latin.

DUCHESS
I did not doubt you, mother.

HECATE
No? What did you?
My power's so firm, it is not be question'd.

DUCHESS
Forgive what's past: and now I know th' offensiveness
That vexes art, I'll shun th' occasion ever.

HECATE
Leave all to me and my five sisters, daughter.
It shall be convey'd in at howlet-time.
Take you no care; my spirits know their moments:
Raven or screech-owl never fly by th' door
But they call in—I thank 'em—and they lose not by't.
I give 'em barley soaked in infants' blood;
They shall have semina cum sanguine,

Their gorge cramm'd full, if they come once to our house.
We are no niggard.

FIRESTONE
They fare but too well when they come hither: they eat up as much tother night as would have made me a good conscionable pudding.

[Exit **DUCHESS**.

HECATE
Give me some lizard's brain, quickly, Firestone.
Where's Grannam Stadlin and all the rest o' th' sisters?

FIRESTONE
All at hand, forsooth.

[Enter **STADLIN, HOPPO**, and the **WITCHES**.

HECATE
Give me marmaritin, some bear-breech; when!

FIRESTONE
Here's bear-breech, and lizard's brain, forsooth.

HECATE
Into the vessel;
And fetch three ounces of the red-hair'd girl
I kill'd last midnight.

FIRESTONE
Whereabouts, sweet mother?

HECATE
Hip; hip or flank. Where is the acopus?

FIRESTONE
You shall have acopus, forsooth.

HECATE
Stir, stir about, whilst I begin the charm.

[A charm song about a vessel.

HECATE
Black spirits and white, red spirits and grey,
Mingle, mingle, mingle, you that mingle may.
Titty, Tiffin, keep it stiff in.
Firedrake, Puckey, make it lucky.

Liard, Robin, you must bob in.
Round, around, around, about, about,
All ill come running in, all good keep out.

FIRST WITCH
Here's the blood of a bat.

HECATE: Put in that, oh, put in that.

SECOND WITCH
Here's libbard's bane.

HECATE
Put in again.

FIRST WITCH
The juice of toad, the oil of adder.

SECOND WITCH
Those will make the younker madder.

HECATE
Put in; there's all, and rid the stench.

FIRESTONE
Nay, here's three ounces of the red-hair'd wench.

ALL
Round, around, around, about, about,
All ill come running in, all good keep out.

HECATE
So, so, enough: into the vessel with it.
There, 't hath the true perfection: I am so light
At any mischief; there's no villainy
But is a tune, methinks.

FIRESTONE [Aside]
A tune? 'Tis to the tune of damnation then, I warrant you, and that song hath a villainous burthen.

HECATE
Come, my sweet sisters, let the air strike our tune
Whilst we show reverence to yond peeping moon.

[Here they dance. The **WITCHES** dance and exit.

Enter Lord **GOVERNOR, ISABELLA, SEBASTIAN** disguised, **FLORIDA, FRANCISCA, ABBERZANES, GASPERO** and other **SERVANTS**.

ISABELLA
My lord, I have given you nothing but the truth
Of a most plain and innocent intent.
My wrongs being so apparent in this woman—
A creature that robs wedlock of all comfort
Where'er she fastens—I could do no less
But seek means privately to shame his folly;
No farther reach'd my malice, and it glads me
That none but my base injurer is found
To be my false accuser.

GOVERNOR
This is strange
That he should give the wrongs, yet seek revenge.
[To **SEBASTIAN**] But, sirrah, you: you are accus'd here doubly,
First by your lady for a false intelligence
That caus'd her absence, which much hurts her name,
Though her intents were blameless; next, by this woman,
For an adulterous design and plot
Practis'd between you to entrap her honour,
Whilst she for her hire should enjoy her husband.
Your answer?

SEBASTIAN
Part of this is truth, my lord,
To which I am guilty, in a rash intent,
But clear in act; and she most clear in both,
Not sanctity more spotless.

[Enter **HERMIO**.

HERMIO
Oh, my lord!

GOVERNOR
What news breaks there?

HERMIO
Of strange destruction:
Here stands the lady that within this hour
Was made a widow.

GOVERNOR

Who?

HERMIO
Your niece, my lord.
A fearful, unexpected accident
Brought death to meet his fury: for my lord
Entering Fernando's house like a rais'd tempest,
Which nothing heeds but its own violent rage,
Blinded with wrath and jealousy, which scorn guides,
From a false trap-door fell into a depth
Exceeds a temple's height, which takes into it
Part of the dungeon that falls threescore faddom
Under the castle.

GOVERNOR
Oh, you seed of lust,
Wrongs and revenges wrongful, with what terrors
You do present yourselves to wretched man,
When his soul least expects you?

ISABELLA
I forgive him
All his wrongs now, and sign it with my pity.

FLORIDA [Swooning]
Oh, my sweet servant!

GOVERNOR
Look to yond light mistress.

GASPERO
She's in a swoon, my lord.

GOVERNOR
Convey her hence;
It is a sight would grieve a modest eye
To see a strumpet's soul sink into passion
For him that was the husband of another.

[Exeunt **SERVANTS** carrying **FLORIDA**.

[To **SEBASTIAN**] Yet all this clears not you.

SEBASTIAN
Thanks to heaven
That I am now of age to clear myself then.

[He removes his disguise.

GOVERNOR
Sebastian?

SEBASTIAN
The same, much wrong'd, sir.

ISABELLA
Am I certain
Of what mine eye takes joy to look upon?

SEBASTIAN
Your service cannot alter me from knowledge.
I am your servant ever.

GOVERNOR
Welcome to life, sir.
Gasper, thou swor'st his death.

GASPERO
I did indeed, my lord,
And have been since well paid for't: one forsworn mouth
Hath got me two or three more here.

SEBASTIAN
I was dead, sir,
Both to my joys and all men's understanding
Till this my hour of life: for 'twas my fortune
To make the first of my return to Urbin
A witness to that marriage, since which time
I have walk'd beneath myself and all my comforts
Like one on earth whose joys are laid above,
And though it had been offence small in me
To enjoy mine own, I left her pure and free.

GOVERNOR
The greater and more sacred is thy blessing,
For where heaven's bounty holy groundwork finds,
'Tis like a sea, encompassing chaste minds.

[Enter **DUCHESS**.

HERMIO
The Duchess comes, my lord.

GOVERNOR
Be you then all witnesses
Of an intent most horrid.

DUCHESS [Aside]
One poor night ever Almachildes now:
Better his meaner fortunes wept than ours
That took the true height of a princess' spirit
To match unto their greatness. Such lives as his
Were only made to break the force of fate
Ere it came at us, and receive the venom.
'Tis but a usual friendship for a mistress
To lose some forty years' life in hopeful time
And hazard an eternal soul forever,
As young as he has done, and more desertful.

GOVERNOR
Madam.

DUCHESS
My lord.

GOVERNOR
This is the hour that I have so long desir'd.
The tumult's full appeas'd: now may we both
Exchange embraces with a fortunate arm
And practise to make love-knots, thus.

[The **DUKE** is discover'd lying on a couch as if dead.

DUCHESS
My lord?

GOVERNOR
Thus, lustful woman and bold murderess, thus.
Blessed powers, to make my loyalty and truth so happy!
Look thee, thou shame of greatness, stain of honour:
Behold thy work and weep before thy death!
If thou beest bless'd with sorrow and a conscience,
Which is a gift from heaven, and seldom knocks
At any murderer's breast with sounds of comfort,
See this thy worthy and unequall'd piece,
A fair encouragement for another husband.

DUCHESS
Bestow me upon death, sir; I am guilty,
And of a cruelty above my cause.
His injury was too low for my revenge.
Perform a justice that may light all others
To noble actions: life is hateful to me,
Beholding my dead lord. Make us an one

In death, whom marriage made one of two living
Till cursed fury parted us. My lord,
I covet to be like him.

GOVERNOR
No, my sword
Shall never stain the virgin brightness on't
With blood of an adulteress.

DUCHESS
There, my lord,
I dare my accuser and defy the world,
Death, shame, and torment: blood, I am guilty of,
But not adultery, not the breach of honour.

GOVERNOR
No? Come forth, Almachildes.

[Enter **ALMACHILDES**.

DUCHESS [Aside]
Almachildes?
Hath time brought him about to save himself
By my destruction? I am justly doom'd.

GOVERNOR
Do you know this woman?

ALMACHILDES
I have known her better, sir, than at this time.

GOVERNOR
But she defies you there.

ALMACHILDES
That's the common trick of them all.

DUCHESS
Nay, since I am touch'd so near: before my death, then,
In right of honour's innocence, I am bold
To call heaven and my woman here to witness.

[Enter **AMORETTA**.

My lord, let her speak truth, or may she perish.

AMORETTA
Then, sir, by all the hopes of a maid's comfort,

Either in faithful service or bless'd marriage,
The woman that his blinded folly knew
Was only a hired strumpet, a professor
Of lust and impudence, which here is ready
To approve what I have spoken.

ALMACHILDES
A common strumpet?
This comes of scarfs; I'll never more wear
An haberdasher's shop before mine eyes again.

GOVERNOR
My sword is proud; thou art lighten'd of that sin.
Die then a murderess only.

DUKE [Rising]
Live a Duchess,
Better than ever lov'd, embraced and honour'd.

DUCHESS
My lord?

DUKE
Nay, since in honour thou canst justly rise,
Vanish all wrongs; thy former practise dies.
I thank thee, Almachildes, for my life,
This lord for truth, and heaven for such a wife,
Who, though her intent sinn'd, yet she makes amends
With grief and honour, virtue's noblest ends.
What griev'd you then shall never more offend you:
Your father's skull with honour we'll inter
And give the peace due to the sepulcher.
And in all time, may this day ever prove
A day of triumph, joy, and honest love.

[Exeunt **OMNES**.

Thomas Middleton – A Short Biography

Thomas Middleton was born in London in April 1580 and baptised on 18th April. He was the son of a bricklayer who had raised himself to the status of a gentleman and become the owner of property adjoining the Curtain Theatre in Shoreditch.

Middleton was aged only five when his father died. His mother remarried but this new union unfortunately fell apart and turned into a fifteen year legal conflict centered on the inheritance of Thomas and his younger sister.

Middleton went on to attend Queen's College, Oxford, matriculating in 1598. However he failed to graduate for reasons unknown leaving either in 1600 or 1601. He had by that time written and published three long poems in popular Elizabethan styles. None appears to have been commercially successful although Microcynicon: Six Snarling Satirese was denounced by the Archbishop of Canterbury and publicly burned as part of his attack on verse satire. Although a minor work, the poems show the roots of Middleton's interest in, and later mature work on, sin, hypocrisy, and lust.

In the early years of the 17th century, Middleton made a living writing topical pamphlets, including one, Penniless Parliament of Threadbare Poets, that was reprinted several times as well as becoming the subject of a parliamentary inquiry.

For one so young he was already making quite an impact and had obviously attracted the eye of the authorities in those turbulent times.

Records surviving of the great theatrical entrepreneur of the day, Philip Henslowe, confirm that Middleton was writing for Henslowe's Admiral's Men. His lauded contemporary, a certain William Shakespeare, was writing only for Henslowe whereas Middleton remained a free agent and able to write for whichever theatrical company hired him.

These early years writing plays continued to attract controversy. His friendship and writing partnership with Thomas Dekker brought him into conflict with Ben Jonson and George Chapman in the so-called War of the Theatres. (This controversy was also called the Poetomachia by Thomas Dekker. The Bishops Ban of 1599 had removed any use of satire from prose and verse publications and so the only outlet was on the stage. For the next 3 years Ben Jonson and George Chapman on one side and John Marston, Thomas Dekker and Thomas Middleton on the other poked fun at their opposition with characters from their plays. The grudge against Jonson continued as late as 1626, when Jonson's play The Staple of News indulges in a slur on Middleton's last play, A Game at Chess).

In 1603, Middleton married. It was also a momentous year in other respects. On the death of Elizabeth I, her cousin James VI of Scotland was now also crowned King James I of England. Another outbreak of the plague now forced the theatres in London to close.

For Middleton the changeover from Elizabethan to Jacobean was the beginning of a long period of success as a writer.

When the theatres re-opened and welcomed back audiences in need of entertainment Middleton was there, writing for several different companies. In particular he specialised in city comedy and revenge tragedy.

During this time he appears also to have written with Shakespeare and he is variously attributed as collaborating on All's Well That Ends Well and Timon of Athens.

Although Middleton had started as a junior partner to Thomas Dekker he was now his fully fledged equal. His finest work with Dekker was undoubtedly The Roaring Girl, a biography of the notorious contemporary thief Mary Frith (Frith began her criminal career as a pickpocket before moving on to highway robbery with a penchant for dressing up as a man. A spell in prison was followed by a long career as a 'fence' from her shop in Fleet St. She lived to the then quite extraordinary age of 74.) The writing is noteworthy not only for its playwriting ambition but in producing a fully formed heroine in Moll Cutpurse. This was only shortly after the role of women in plays had seen fit to have them played, in the main, by men.

In the 1610s, Middleton began another playwriting partnership, this time with the actor William Rowley, producing another slew of plays including the classics Wit at Several Weapons and A Fair Quarrel.

The ever adaptable Middleton seemed at ease working with others or by himself. His solo writing credits include the comic masterpiece, A Chaste Maid in Cheapside, in 1613. Interestingly his solo plays are somewhat less thrusting and bellicose. Certainly there is no comedy among them with the satirical depth of Michaelmas Term and no tragedy as raw, striking and as bloodthirsty as The Revenger's Tragedy.

There may be various reasons for this and among them that he was increasingly involved with civic pageants and therefore was trying to avoid too much controversy especially without the cover of a collaborator. Indeed in 1620, he was officially appointed as chronologer of the City of London, a post he held until his death in 1627, when ironically, it passed to his great rival, and sometime enemy, Ben Jonson.

Middleton's official duties did not interrupt his dramatic writing; the 1620s saw the production of his and Rowley's tragedy, and continual favourite, The Changeling, as well as several other tragicomedies.

However in 1624, he reached a peak of notoriety when his dramatic allegory A Game at Chess was staged by the King's Men. The play used the conceit of a chess game to present and satirise the recent intrigues surrounding the Spanish Match; James I's son, Prince Charles, was being positioned to marry the daughter, Maria Anna of the Spanish King Philip IV of Spain. Though Middleton's approach was strongly patriotic, the Privy Council closed the play, after only nine performances at the Globe theatre, having received a complaint from the Spanish ambassador. The Privy Council then opened a prosecution against both authors and actors. Although Middleton in his defence showed that the play had been passed by the Master of the Revels, Sir Henry Herbert, any further performance was forbidden and the author and actors fined.

What happened next is a mystery. It is the last play recorded as having being written by Middleton. His playwriting career appears to have stopped dead. It follows that some sort of further punishment probably occurred and for a writer can there be any greater punishment than not being allowed to write or be heard?

Middleton's work is diverse even by the standards of his age. His career Middleton covers many many genres including tragedy, history and city comedy. As we have noted he did not have the kind of official relationship with a particular company that Shakespeare or Fletcher had that might have supported him in a lean creative period. Instead he appears to have written on a freelance basis for any number of companies. His output ranges from the "snarling" satire of Michaelmas Term, performed by the Children of Paul's, to the bleak intrigues of The Revenger's Tragedy, performed by the King's Men. Interestingly earlier editions of The Revenger's Tragedy attributed the play solely to Cyril Tourneur but recent studies have shredded that view so that Middleton's authorship is not now seriously contested

Indeed modern techniques in analysing writing styles are now leaning towards giving Middleton credit for his adaptation and revision of Shakespeare's Macbeth and Measure for Measure. Along with the more established evidence of collaboration on All's Well That Ends Well and Timon of Athens it appears that Middleton has moved some way forward to the front rank of playwrights and an association, in some form, but its greatest exponent.

His early work was informed by the blossoming, in the late Elizabethan period, of satire, while his maturity was influenced by the ascendancy of Fletcherian tragicomedy. Middleton's later work, in which his satirical fury is tempered and broadened, includes three of his acknowledged masterpieces. A Chaste Maid in Cheapside, produced by the Lady Elizabeth's Men, which skillfully combines London life with an expansive view of the power of love to effect reconciliation even though London seems populated entirely by sinners, in which no social rank goes unsatirised. The Changeling, a later tragedy, returns Middleton to an Italianate setting like that of The Revenger's Tragedy, except that here the central characters are more fully drawn and more compelling as individuals. Similar development can be seen in Women Beware Women.

Middleton's plays are marked by their cynicism, though often very funny, about the human race. His characters are complex. True heroes are a rarity: almost all of his characters are selfish, greedy, and self-absorbed.

When Middleton does portray good people, the characters are often presented as flawless and perfect and given small, undemanding roles. A theological pamphlet attributed to Middleton gives sustenance to the notion that Middleton was a strong believer in Calvinism.

Thomas Middleton died at his home at Newington Butts in Southwark in the summer of 1627, and was buried on July 4th, in St Mary's churchyard which today survives as a public park in Elephant and Castle.

Middleton stands with John Fletcher and Ben Jonson as the most successful and prolific of playwrights from the Jacobean period. Very few Renaissance dramatists would achieve equal success in both comedy and tragedy but Middleton was one. He also wrote many masques and pageants and remains, to this day, one of the most notable of Jacobean dramatists.

Middleton's work has long been praised by many literary critics, among the most fervent were Algernon Charles Swinburne and T. S. Eliot. The latter thought Middleton was second only to Shakespeare.

Among their contemporaries was a very crowded field of talent including: Ben Jonson (1572-1637), Christopher Marlowe (1564-1593), Francis Beaumont (1585-1616), Henry Chettle (1564-1606), John Fletcher (1579–1625), John Ford (1586–1639), John Day (1574-1640), John Marston (1576-1634), John Webster (1580-1634), Nathan Field (1587-1620), Philip Massinger (1584-1640), Richard Burbage (1567-1619), Robert Greene (1558-1592), Thomas Dekker (1575-1625), Thomas Kyd (1558-1594), William Haughton (died 1605), William Rowley (1585-1626).

It's a daunting list and confirms that to top that made you a very special talent indeed.

Thomas Middleton – A Concise Bibliography

It has long been recognised that the modern concept of authorship was rather more elastic in centuries past. Writers were not only for hire, and their work therefore a commodity, but their plays ran much shorter lengths; two weeks being a common term of performance. To that themes and scenes were liberally excised from one play and used in another. Revisions to past plays that were being restaged would be undertaken and entirely credited to other writers. Many works and plays were unpublished and have not survived and some only from memory by actors etc. Whilst many of these playwrights are only now feted for their talents, some undoubtedly were at the time, but it is difficult to, in every case, to establish exact provenance. With modern scholarly and literary techniques author attributions have sometimes changed or been re-balanced. For those where this may be the case we have placed the *Play's Title and other information* in italics

Plays

Blurt, Master Constable or The Spaniard's Night Walk (with Thomas Dekker (1602)

The Phoenix (1603–4)

The Honest Whore, Part 1, a city comedy (1604), (with Thomas Dekker)

Michaelmas Term, a city comedy, (1604)

All's Well That Ends Well (1604-5); believed by some to be co-written by Middleton based on stylometric analysis.

A Trick to Catch the Old One, a city comedy (1605)

A Mad World, My Masters, a city comedy (1605)

A Yorkshire Tragedy, a one-act tragedy (1605); attributed to Shakespeare on its title page, but stylistic analysis favours Middleton.

Timon of Athens a tragedy (1605–6); stylistic analysis indicates that Middleton may have written this play in collaboration with William Shakespeare.

The Puritan (1606)

The Revenger's Tragedy (1606). Earlier editions often mistakenly attribute authorship to Cyril Tourneur.

Your Five Gallants, a city comedy (1607)

The Family of Love (1607) some attribute this to Middleton others include Dekker and Lording Barry.

The Bloody Banquet (1608–9); co-written with Thomas Dekker.

The Roaring Girl, a city comedy depicting the exploits of Mary Frith (1611); with Thomas Dekker.

No Wit, No Help Like a Woman's, a tragic-comedy (1611)

The Second Maiden's Tragedy, a tragedy (1611); an anonymous manuscript; stylistic analysis indicates Middleton's authorship (though one scholar also attributed it to Shakespeare.

A Chaste Maid in Cheapside, a city comedy (1613)

Wit at Several Weapons, a city comedy (1613); printed as part of the Beaumont and Fletcher Folio, but stylistic analysis indicates comprehensive revision by Middleton & Rowley.

More Dissemblers Besides Women, a tragicomedy (1614)

The Widow (1615–16)

The Witch, a tragicomedy (1616)

A Fair Quarrel, a tragicomedy (1616). Co-written with William Rowley.

The Old Law, a tragicomedy (1618–19). written with William Rowley and perhaps a third collaborator.

Hengist, King of Kent, or The Mayor of Quinborough, a tragedy (1620)

Women Beware Women, a tragedy (1621)

Measure for Measure (1603-4); some scholars argue that the First Folio text was partly revised by Middleton in 1621.

Anything for a Quiet Life, a city comedy (1621). Co-written with John Webster.

The Changeling, a tragedy (1622). Co-written with William Rowley.

The Nice Valour (1622). Printed as part of the Beaumont and Fletcher Folio, but stylistic analysis indicates comprehensive revision by Middleton.

The Spanish Gypsy, a tragicomedy (1623). Believed to be a play by Middleton & Rowley and later revised by Thomas Dekker and John Ford.

A Game at Chess, a political satire (1624). Satirized the negotiations over the proposed marriage of Prince Charles, son of James I of England, with the Spanish princess. Closed after nine performances.

Masques & Entertainments

The Whole Royal and Magnificent Entertainment Given to King James Through the City of London (1603–4). Co-written with Thomas Dekker, Stephen Harrison & Ben Jonson.

The Manner of his Lordship's Entertainment

The Triumphs of Truth

Civitas Amor

The Triumphs of Honour and Industry (1617)

The Masque of Heroes, or, The Inner Temple Masque (1619)

The Triumphs of Love and Antiquity (1619)

The World Tossed at Tennis (1620). Co-written with William Rowley.

Honourable Entertainments (1620–1)

An Invention (1622)

The Sun in Aries (1621)

The Triumphs of Honour and Virtue (1622)

The Triumphs of Integrity with The Triumphs of the Golden Fleece (1623)

The Triumphs of Health and Prosperity (1626)

Poetry

The Wisdom of Solomon Paraphrased (1597)

Microcynicon: Six Snarling Satires (1599)

The Ghost of Lucrece (1600)

Burbage epitaph (1619)

Bolles epitaph (1621)

Duchess of Malfi (commendatory poem) (1623)

St James (1623)

To the King (1624)

Prose

The Penniless Parliament of Threadbare Poets (1601)

News from Gravesend. Co-written with Thomas Dekker (1603)

The Nightingale and the Ant aka Father Hubbard's Tales (1604)

The Meeting of Gallants at an Ordinary (1604). Co-written with Thomas Dekker.

Plato's Cap Cast at the Year 1604 (1604)

The Black Book (1604)

Sir Robert Sherley his Entertainment in Cracovia (1609) (translation).

The Two Gates of Salvation (1609), or The Marriage of the Old and New Testament.

The Owl's Almanac (1618)

The Peacemaker (1618)

CPSIA information can be obtained
at www.ICGtesting.com
Printed in the USA
LVHW021152180121
676576LV00012BA/1486

9 781785 438776